THE HIGDON CHRONICLES

Iron Butts, Airheads, and My Life Behind Bars

VOLUME ONE

Robert E. Higdon

Cover photograph: The road to Magdagachi, Siberia, July 2004
(Robert E. Higdon)

Editor: Jerry Smith, JerrySmithAuthor.com

Design and production of cover and interior: Marcella Fox,
MarcellaFox.com

Cover fonts: Diamante and Humana Serif ITC
Interior fonts: Diamante and Marion

Contents

On Radio 4 last night there was some stuff about psych profiling and the origins of that particular form of witch-craft. Turns out, in the late '30s and early '40s, the RAF developed a system for profiling potential fighter pilots to go up against the Luftwaffe's finest.

Question 1. Do you enjoy riding motorcycles?

Question 2. Do you currently ride motorcycles?

Apparently the perfect answers were 1. Yes and 2. No. The basis is that they wanted kids who were brave enough to enjoy riding motorcycles, but not crazy enough to keep doing it.

We would have failed the test.

Paul Allison
Email to the author
February 2019

The impulse to memorialize in book form transient essays scattered around in periodicals is an impulse that should be suppressed. It should be but seldom is.

Jacob A. Stein

Acknowledgements

More than 20 years ago I first typed "Acknowledgements" for what would become this book. My resistance to finishing the project has been, I'm convinced, a belief that when you saw such a compilation — Frankie Avalon's Greatest Hits, for example — you were looking at a career headed for the toilet. I wasn't ready for the toilet then. But now? I had my 40th birthday almost 40 years ago. Trust me: There are worse fates than winding up in the loo, even one in Magdagachi, Siberia.

Permit me then to give credit where it is clearly due.

A chance meeting with Joel Rosenthal in the summer of 1985 not only altered the direction of my life but taught me that long-distance motorcycle riding was more a function of the fullness of the rider's heart than the hardness of his ass. Joel rode a BMW model R75/6, which has an air-cooled engine and is the lineal descendant of machines dating back to 1923. Aficionados revere the design and proudly call themselves "Airheads." It is to them and not ditzy blondes I refer in the subtitle of this book.

For 30 years and counting Mike Kneebone, the founder and president of the Iron Butt Association, has been my closest friend, wisest advisor, and sanest psychiatrist.

Tim and Coral Moffitt in Colorado and Shane, Karen, and Sandy Smith in Mississippi have given me homes away from home almost since dirt was new.

Susan Carhart and I shared my house in Washington, D.C., for 25 years. Little that I wrote during that time saw the light of day without her approval.

More than 50 years ago Christine Jorgensen, née Haglund,

and I met while working in the new field of computer programming. We reunited, as Gilbert & Sullivan might say, by a set of curious chances in 2011. I have a spectacular imagination, but I cannot imagine a life without Chris providing adult supervision to me.

This book would not exist without the outrageous patience over 12 years of my editor, Jerry Smith. It is one thing to write and another to correct. He does both, and superbly. I am also deeply indebted to Jerry and Bill Watt for the book's title, one that Oscar Wilde himself might have envied.

One acknowledgement remains. The contents of this book represent the intersection of two of my life's passions, long-distance travel and motorcycles. The former began on a cross-country automobile trip when I was six years old and the latter as a consequence of Dickensian poverty and hideous choices during college.

Motorcyclists represent about 2 percent of road traffic. For reasons that escape me still, I was attracted by a subset of such people, the cohort who rode the big miles. This, I supposed, was maybe 2 percent of the 2 percent of motorists on the road. Jonathan Swift's poem came to mind:

> *So, naturalists observe, a flea*
> *Hath smaller fleas that on him prey;*
> *And these have smaller still to bite 'em;*
> *And so proceed ad infinitum.*

George Wyman started it in 1903, riding a motorcycle from San Francisco to New York in 51 days. Not to be outdone, nine years later Carl Stearns Clancy rode a bike around the world. Thus did the globe-trotting gates open: Robert Fulton, Danny and Arlene Liska, Ted Simon, Helge Pedersen, Steve and Debra Attwood, Jim Rogers, Simon Milward, Greg Frazier, and nameless others. Scores, maybe hundreds or more, are out there this minute, working without a net for years at a time.

For those world travelers the motorcycle was, or is, their only job. Others, cursed with the same desire to be on the road, have had to organize their riding lives around their working lives. In 1984 Mike Rose, a New Jersey motorcycle-accessories dealer, provided a competitive outlet for them. He created the Iron Butt Rally, advertised as a 10-day scavenger hunt by motorcycle across North America. Rose's idea was eventually taken up by Mike Kneebone and the Iron Butt Association was born. Without putting too fine a point on it, these are the people your mother warned you about.

Merely leaving the driveway for a trip to the grocery store on a motorcycle demands a lot. You balance the bike with your inner ears and operate the clutch, gas, and brakes with two hands and two feet. Now consider riding long distances night and day in sub-optimal conditions. That's the dark domain of the flea's flea, a second order of smallness. There aren't many people that tiny. They are the Iron Butts, gunslingers of the motorcycle world, and a true breed apart. I call them the last cowboys and it is to them I dedicate this book.

If this strikes you as incomprehensible, have no fear. I don't understand it myself, and I am one of them.

Introduction

In the spring of 1946 my father, an army physician, received orders directing him to proceed from the Greenbrier Hotel — then owned and operated by the War Department as a general hospital in White Sulfur Springs, West Virginia — to Letterman General Hospital in San Francisco, California. Our family of four piled into a pre-war Chevrolet and headed west.

I was six, not too old apparently to have my brain indelibly imprinted with the constantly changing scenery. This wasn't an adventure every day but one every 10 minutes. Plains, rivers, mountains, and deserts appeared and receded. When we reached California I asked when we might do that again.

Soon, thank God. Our relatives were concentrated in two small towns in the deep South. In the summers of 1948 and 1950 we were back in the car, hammering day and night from San Francisco to McComb, Mississippi. Take a look at a map. That's a 2,200-mile hike, half of it on what was then U.S. Route 66. I was 10 years old and already knew the Mother Road like a long-haul trucker. A 10-year-old travel junkie.

In 1953 we began a three-year tour in Tokyo, then returned to Walter Reed Hospital in Washington, D.C., where both my brother and I had been born. The move back to the U.S. did not suit me. I was entering my senior year of high school. I'd loved Japan. I was not loving D.C. one bit. I graduated, barely, and entered college in the fall of 1957, angry and ready for trouble.

I found it quickly. Before the end of October that year Jack Kerouac's *On the Road* and Ayn Rand's *Atlas Shrugged* were published. Parents of confused, 17-year-old boys, hear me: You cannot let your son near such material. Give him a Glock and some ammo. Give him a bottle of whiskey and the car keys. He'll be better off.

I lasted one semester and withdrew. I returned, majoring in beer and poker. In the spring of 1959 I flunked out for the first time. By now you couldn't reach me with a radio telescope. But for the toe tag, I was dead at 19, unable to have outlived even Billy the Kid. And those were the good years.

In the fall of 1962, a year beyond the point when I should have graduated from college, I was living on a couch in a fraternity house in College Park, Maryland. My marriage at the beginning of the semester hadn't made it to homecoming weekend. I scraped a few hundred dollars together, bought a used Vespa motor scooter, and rode it down to my parents' quarters in Fort Eustis, Virginia, for Thanksgiving. My father was the commandant of the hospital on the post, his last assignment for the army. I'd neglected to tell them that since we'd last been together I'd gotten married, my wife was seven months pregnant, and absent divine intervention I was almost certain to fail each and every course I was taking, including volleyball. I also mentioned that my father-in-law had arranged to have me thrown in jail the month before for non-support but I was pretty sure I had that under control. Pass the turkey, please.

The look of inexpressible pain in my mother's eyes that morning is with me still. I'd finally reached the bottom, the realm where the 12-step programs kick in. For five years I'd slammed every door and torched every bridge in sight. The climb out of the pit wouldn't be easy.

Ironically, the laughably dangerous Vespa, having spent every day of its vicious life trying to deliver me to a morgue, became the literal vehicle of my salvation. It freed me from dependency on a bus, hitchhiking, or my feet. It took me to jobs, to classes, and finally to a graduation ceremony in August, 1965, nearly eight years after I'd begun. I sold the Vespa and bought a real motorcycle, the first of 41 I would own over the years.

After that, life became a proverbial stroll through a garden. I began to notice a correlation between hard work and good fortune. Steps were climbed: first a computer programmer, then a law student, and finally a lawyer, stumbling into a dream position with ridiculous ease. Mercifully, before Alzheimer's took her away, my mother saw her elder son no longer at war with himself.

Still, the absence of war does not necessarily mean peace. I was never going to have much of that. The constant presence of a bike in the garage was the guarantee: People who ride motorcycles cannot help themselves, and motorcycles cannot help but bring a world of downside risks.

As I mentioned in the Acknowledgements above, my meeting Joel Rosenthal was a game changer. There was an invisible world of long-distance riders who were doing what I'd wanted to do since I first crawled into that Chevrolet in 1946. Dominoes began to fall almost by script. I met Mike Kneebone in March 1989 and a month later joined the BMW Bikers of Metropolitan Washington (BMWBMW). In 1991 we combined forces with the American Motorcyclist Association (AMA) to win an epic battle that opened up high-occupancy-vehicle lanes to motorcycles in Virginia. I was named AMA's Road Rider of the Year in 1992 for that effort, though in all candor the honor should have been shared with at least three other attorneys.

During that time I crossed paths with Robert Hellman, the most literate and cultured man I've ever known. He was the editor of *On the Level*, the magazine of the BMW Riders Association, a national club. He asked that I write a column for him. I did, 164 of them in the next 18 years named *The View from the Bunker*. His death in 2008 gutted me. Simultaneously, I felt BMW had completely lost its way. Its bikes had become unreliable, it was eliminating dealerships, and its market share — never more than anemic — was being hammered further. When my last BMW broke down 3,000 miles from home in 2009, I sold it. In 37 years I'd bought 31 of their machines and had racked up over a million miles. I said goodbye, but I didn't wave.

The more deeply I immersed myself in motorcycles, the more I wanted to stop practicing law. Toward the end the only part of the job I enjoyed was the travel. I kept a stable of expert medical witnesses in Southern California for the sole purpose of enabling me to fly across the country, confer with them for an hour, retrieve a bike I garaged in Redondo Beach, and ride around for a week. That tail could wag the dog for only so long. On July 31, 1992, I locked my office on K Street in Washington, D.C., for the last time and retired. I was 52.

At last the two great loves of my life, motorcycles and a road upon which to ride them, were aligned. The six-year-old boy was ready to head out once more. Believe me: If you're able to do and enjoy as an adult what you enjoyed doing as a kid, you'll have realized the dream.

Bob Higdon
Daytona Beach, Florida
March 2019

Mariposa

PHOTO CREDIT: BILL SHAW

BMW Mileage Award medallion

We've all heard someone say, "When I woke up that morning, I didn't know my life was about to change." But the mere act of waking up pretty much guarantees that *something* different will happen that day, doesn't it? Still, May 24, 1986, was a day that seriously altered my life, though it was far from clear to me when I woke up that Saturday just how dramatic the change would be.

I'd flown to Sacramento from the east coast a day earlier to take the deposition of a witness in a medical malpractice case. For me that was always the fun part (the travel, not listening to yet another perjurer trying to dig a grave for my client). By noon the bloodletting had ceased. I walked out to the parking lot, trying to remember what my rental car looked like. One moment I thought I'd return to San Francisco; the next moment I was driving south and east to Mariposa in the foothills of the Sierra Nevada mountains. That's how it started.

Permit me to backtrack a moment. For the first 25 years of my moto life, I was the very definition of a lone rider. I knew no motorcyclists, belonged to no clubs, and subscribed to no bike magazines. Since my annual mileage rarely exceeded 1,500, I'd take my thudding, pile-driving pig of a '79 R65 to the nearest BMW dealer once a year for an oil change. If something was happening in the world of two wheels, I'd hear about it through the drums or not at all.

In August 1985, however, I met Joel. He'd seen my bike parked on the street in Cabin John, Maryland. Like a junkyard dog sensing an intruder, he rode over to investigate. His machine was an R75/6, though even that was hard to determine because of the dirt, tar, mud, bugs, and spooge that slathered the machine on all exposed surfaces from stem to stern and guggle to zatch. Compared to that unholy specimen, my R65, no jewel itself, belonged in the Louvre.

"Joel Rosenthal," he said, sticking out his hand.

I admitted who I was. "Looks like you've been riding," I said wanly.

"Came in from Great Falls yesterday."

"Montana?" I asked, stunned. His machine didn't look capable of making it from Great Falls, Maryland, three miles up the road.

"Four days," he smiled.

"Four *Earth* days?" I smiled back.

"I've got the gas receipts," he said unsmiling. As I would learn over the next 20 years, Joel was many things, but he was not a liar.

Within an hour everything I thought I knew about motorcycles lay in the dust between our bikes. I felt like one of Plato's cave dwellers who'd spent a lifetime seeing nothing but reflected shadows on a dimly lit wall. Now I was being escorted into the sunlight by an unusual guide.

"And join this BMW MOA club," he advised. "They've got a book with telephone numbers you can call when you break down. They have a monthly magazine too." A year later it was that magazine I was thumbing through during lulls in the Sacramento deposition, and noticing an announcement for a motorcycle rally that weekend down the road in Mariposa.

California Highway 49, as its name suggests, has its origins in the '49er trails from the Gold Rush days. Traveled by Mark Twain, Bret Harte, and jumping frogs of Calaveras County, it is one of the West's great motorcycle routes. Even in a rental car that sways and lurches through the endless corners like a sotted mule, it's a trip to remember. For certain, it's the road you'll take when you head to Mariposa on a spring afternoon and want to change your life.

It never occurred to me to call for a motel reservation. Having never been to a rally, I hadn't the vaguest clue that a thousand people would be overwhelming the tiny town, itself home to not more than a thousand people. So when I checked in to the last available room at the Best Western, I wasn't even surprised at my good luck. It's the air of entitlement that European travelers carry with them like a St. Christopher medal. They expect good fortune, and good fortune magically appears. In the shower I scrubbed off the blood and duplicity from the deposition and headed for the main street. In Mariposa there's only one.

I had never seen so many BMW motorcycles. It was as if I'd stumbled into the atrium of a hive. They lined both sides of the street, bikes of every stripe, configuration, accoutrement, and hue. I felt like a latter-day Columbus, but a wanderer found, not lost. One old bike, a shell-shocked beater by any definition, had backed in toward the curb. Attached to its rear fender was a small medallion. I looked at it more closely. It read: "100,000 Mile BMW Award."

I almost recoiled from the machine. *Excuse me? This guy can do 100 large ones on a motorcycle, a bike older than my own R65 swine maiden?* I checked the odometer: 60K and change. So they were cumulative miles. Still, it was a lot of zeroes. I'd been riding BMWs for 15 years by that point and didn't have nearly that many. I walked away. Bikes buzzed by, racking up lifetime miles between the restaurant and the Best Western. Within the space of five minutes I'd abandoned my dream of winning a Nobel prize in quantum astrostringphysics. My life's new ambition was to scam one of those medallions. Before I came to Mariposa, I didn't know what I didn't know. When I left, I could see a path.

But a little knowledge is worse than dangerous. It often leads to a little more. Within a year I was on a K75, moving from the most blighted motorcycle BMW ever made to the very best. Gradually and fitfully in that pre-internet darkness,

I became aware of an endurance-riding sub-culture, populated by people who had lots of BMW mileage awards, but a group so involuted as to exist principally by telepathy. We were a perfect match: I could tell their twisted story; they could catch me when I fell. We've been doing both ever since.

Though it sometimes seems that a geologic era has passed since that weekend in the Sierras, I think of it often. The links in the chain, from that first meeting with Joel until today, are seamless. Mariposa, the Spanish word for "butterfly," is the master link. The town's name implies metamorphosis: I was that, and now I'm this. Yesterday I crawled; today I fly. Tomorrow, if I'm lucky and God is willing, I may become something else.

The Hook

Aerostich CEO Andy Goldfine

The mind of a writer can be a truly terrifying
thing. Isolated, neurotic, caffeine-addled,
crippled by procrastination, consumed by
feelings of panic, self-loathing, and soul-crushing
inadequacy. And that's on a good day.

— *Robert de Niro, Academy of Motion Picture Arts and
Sciences Oscar presentation for best original and adapted
screenplays, March 2, 2014.*

To celebrate the 30th anniversary of the founding of the
Aerostich company, Andy Goldfine invited friends, family,
and fans to Duluth, Minnesota, at the end of August last year
for the third iteration — he's been putting on this event at five-
year intervals since 2003 — of the Very Boring Rally. Included
in the rally package was a list of things to see in the area,
notably the boyhood home of Bobby Zimmerman at 519 N. 3rd
Avenue E. I rode over to take a look. The house is a duplex,
clinging gamely to a fairly steep slope. Lake Superior sits at the
bottom of the hill to the southeast. I shut down the motor and
stared at the house.

"This is it," I thought. "The hook. Two dudes from Duluth.
Zimmerman, the guy who can't keep a motorcycle upright, and
Goldfine, the guy who treats bikes as a transformative personal
and social good. It's perfect. The conflict is built-in. The story
will write itself." And it did, though it took six months and
produced more than a little soul-crushing inadequacy. But I
see that I am a bit ahead of myself. I need to explain a couple
of things.

First, the hook. If you take a motorcycle ride and write a story about your adventure, you need to tell your readers more than what you paid for gas and how the eggs were cooked at Mom's Café. That's what is wrong with all the worthless touring stories that appear in motorcycle club newsletters and magazines. There's no hook, nothing to grab the reader and say, "Here, *this* is what makes my ride unique." Every good story, from a half-hour television comedy to the King James Bible, snares the audience.

Second, Bobby Zimmerman. That was his name before he reinvented himself as Bob Dillon (later Bob Dylan), moved to New York, and became part of the Greenwich Village folk-music scene in 1961. He would be my bad dude in counterpoint to Goldfine, my good dude. There's the hook: a modern western with Duluth as a seminal O.K. Corral, guy in black hat, guy in white hat, and motorcycles instead of horses. Nothing to it.

Making a villain out of the youthful Bob Dylan was child's play. On arriving in New York he immediately began erasing all ties to his middle-class background, telling gullible interviewers that he'd traveled with the circus for six years, struggled with a $25/day heroin habit, and worked occasionally as a male whore. He treated friends shabbily, but he had raw talent and finally got his wish. The curly-haired kid from N. 3rd Avenue E became famous. Then on July 29, 1966, near Woodstock, New York, he crashed his two-year old Triumph T100, a cut-down version of the 650 Bonneville.

Over the years he told at least three versions of how the accident happened. The simple truth was that his motorcycle skills were not much. Joan Baez wrote that Dylan "used to hang on that thing like a sack of flour." He most likely had been starting out on cold, underinflated tires and crashed in the first 50 feet. Although he claimed that he'd shattered several cervical vertebrae and was in critical condition for a week, no cop or ambulance was called. He was taken not to a hospital but to the home of a hippie physician who specialized in keeping the press away from his patient for the next six weeks. The wreck gave Dylan time to restructure a life that had been spiraling wildly out of control for several years. He told an interviewer, "I probably would have died if I had kept on going the way I had been." He would not go back on tour for eight years.

Painting Andy Goldfine as a righteous cowboy was equally easy. He has spent his adult life trying to keep motorcyclists in one piece, so to speak. In 1982 he acquired some industrial-strength sewing machines, fit only for producing outdoor clothing like snowmobile suits. So what do you get when you take a college philosophy major who rides a bike and owns a bunch of sewing machines? The iconic Roadcrafter one-piece riding suit. Although designed as utilitarian commuter wear, it was quickly adopted by the motorcycle press corps and by a more adventurous and determined audience. "I get photos from riders at the four corners of everywhere," Andy says. "I'd be just as happy if they were riding the suits to work." Be that as it may, the modern symbol of the long-distance rider, John Ryan, was so inextricably identified with the Roadcrafter that he was laid to rest in one last fall.

For Goldfine it's always been about more than selling stuff. He really believes that riding a bike makes you a healthier, happier, more well-adjusted person. He will go on endlessly about dopamine and endorphin secretions. He gets excited. His eyes light up. He's his own ShamWow commercial. But wait! There's more! Riding a bike isn't easy. Ask Bobby Zimmerman. Both hands and both feet operate in an intricate, sophisticated dance. All five senses are on alert. The brain and the ass and everything else battle for control. Pull this trick off — actually guide the two-wheeled bitch to a finish where and when you want to — and you're a self-validated genius. No wonder you feel so damned good.

I tossed in a final paragraph about Dylan spending his life blowin' in the wind and singing the same song two hundred million times, while Andy's times were always a-changin'. Cheap tropes, of course, but easy. The column was in the bag. I emailed it to Bill Shaw and Mike Kneebone with a note: "I've sent it to Andy for fact checking, but I think he'll sign off."

He didn't quite. He mentioned in a return email that he and Dylan are first cousins once removed. I felt a little queasy. It got worse. The duplex where the Zimmermans lived on N. 3rd Avenue E was owned by Andy's grandparents. Ouch. And maybe I was being a little rough on the young Bob D. Sure, he was telling some tall tales in the early days, but if you're 19 and desperate to be noticed, you'll say anything. I stopped reading and called Andy. We talked for 40 minutes. I wasn't trying to save my story. I knew it was atomic dust. My entire concept had been premised on smacking an ambitious kid eager to make it in the toughest racket imaginable, a guy who would rewrite the history of American music. He had a dumb bike crash and was embarrassed about it; like I haven't, again and again. Fifty-something albums in 50-plus years. Dust. Every word was dust.

We hung up. Why hadn't he told those of us at the rally about the history of the Zimmermans and Goldfines? I shook my head. Not his style. By now I'm feeling a little neurotic. The deadline was days ago and I need a new hook. Panic. Self-loathing. How could I have gone so wrong? Stay calm. Crank up an MP3 album. Hmm. *Nashville Skyline*. Hard to find anything better than that. This will work out. It always does. Need some caffeine.

Giants and Ghosts

PHOTO CREDIT: DETAIL FROM BACK COVER OF LISKA'S BOOK, *TWO WHEELS TO ADVENTURE*

Danny Liska and his co-rider

Twenty motorcycles were already parked in front of the Two Rivers Saloon and Hotel in Niobrara, Nebraska, when I arrived. Another 20 would appear before the cold, wet day ended. We had gathered in this tiny town in the middle of the Great Plains to meet the past and the legends who inhabited it.

Geographers know Niobrara as both one of Nebraska's oldest towns — Lewis and Clark camped in the area at the confluence of the Missouri and Niobrara rivers — and its newest, having twice been relocated to higher ground following flooding by the Missouri. Motorcyclists know it as the ancestral home of Danny Liska, who, as a result of some truly remarkable globe-trotting rides, was featured in ad campaigns for BMW bikes in the 1960s.

His story was, as he knew it would be, Hollywood drama at its finest: In 1959 a young Nebraska farmer leaves behind his wife, Arlene, to take care of the cattle, buys a BMW street bike, and heads off to Alaska, more than 3,200 miles away. Sticking the front wheel in the Yukon river, he then points the battered machine toward Ushuaia at the very bottom of South America. Along the way he hikes through the Darien jungle between Panama and Colombia and works as a stand-in for Yul Brynner during the filming of the movie *Taras Bulba* in Argentina.

Home again in Niobrara after tens of thousands of miles, he could have rested, knowing that few men in motorcycling had ever accomplished as much. But rest was the last thing on his mind. He negotiated the purchase of a new R60 through Butler & Smith, then the importers of BMW bikes to the

U.S., and took delivery of it in Germany from Schorsch Meier, another hero of the BMW marque. Between September 1963 and November 1964, Liska paralleled his earlier ride, this time from the top of Norway to the bottom of Africa.

Years later he recounted the first half of the odyssey in a self-published book, *Two Wheels to Adventure: Alaska to Argentina by Motorcycle*, almost 800 photo-laden pages of a writing style that mirrored his riding style: straight ahead with blunt force. His world, like his photos, was black and white. If there is even one example of subtlety or nuance in the entire book, I cannot recall it. Still, you put it down with almost palpable relief and a sense that Liska has left nothing on the table.

But he had, and the truth was that in a couple of significant ways, his travels had been vastly different from what he had described.

In the first place, the rides had not been straight shots from one pole to the other but in fact were frequently interrupted by returning home for money, supplies, and energy. He was not a rich man — not many small-scale cattle farmers are — and even modest support from the few sponsors he was able to attract was still years in the future.

Even stranger was the complete absence of Arlene's name in the book. There are a thousand photos, mostly of Danny and spectacular landscapes, but not a single one of her. And yet, except for some brief intervals, she had been riding two-up with Danny on both expeditions almost every mile of the way. What in the world had happened?

Enter the other woman, this one an eerie Colombian mystic with the improbable name of Regina 11. Danny, always a sucker for the supernatural, had met her on one of his passages through the country. Eventually he divorced Arlene, moved to Colombia, married the seer, wrote his book, and in the process eviscerated his former wife's part and presence in their travels.

It was a repudiation of almost Soviet-like coldness, where in the 1930s disfavored party officials found their names removed from history books and their images cut from group photos and replaced by bookcases and lamps. Indeed, a back-cover photo of *Two Wheels to Adventure* shows Danny on the bike with a large parrot. But the bird is a superimposition. If you look carefully, you can just make out the edges of a second rider. It is, or was before the purge, Arlene.

Now 79, but neither looking nor acting her age, Arlene still resides in Niobrara, though the Bigfoot farm where she and Danny lived in happier days was sold out from under her years ago. In the hotel that night, May 12, she did a slide show of her travels in Africa with Danny.

"We picked up the motorcycle in Germany. It didn't run right. When we brought it back to Munich, Mr. Meier said that Danny wasn't operating it properly." A BMW rider in the back of the room said to laughter and cheers, "Some things never change."

Arlene clicks through the slides. They are of uniformly poor quality — Danny and Regina took all the good ones to South America — but there are some of a young, smiling, auburn-haired woman who sits on a motorcycle in the Transvaal on a summer's day. A few years in the future her life will come crashing down around her, but tonight she looks at the fading Kodachrome with a trace of a smile. She loved that man. You can feel it. She loves him still.

Eddie James, the American Motorcyclist Association's director of road riding and one of the usual suspects on the Iron Butt Rally, has dedicated himself to ensuring that Danny and Arlene receive the recognition they deserve for their incredible accomplishments. He might be the son they never had. Though he has seen Arlene's presentation before, he still concentrates on her intently as she speaks, perhaps assisting her with some kind of telepathy that Danny would have appreciated.

She shows us part of a zebra skin and some pelts from long-haired monkeys, handling them tenderly because they and a few other objects are all that she has left and they are literally disintegrating with age. Then, for the first time, her voice catches.

"I told Eddie this might be a difficult night for me," she says softly. "Today is the anniversary of the day that Danny and I were married. And this is the 10th anniversary of the day that he died."

He was a large man, and it would take something equally large to kill him. Leukemia did it. He wanted to be sent off like a Viking, incinerated on a pyre. Regina saw that it was done. It broke Arlene's heart.

But five years before his death I had had a chance to meet Danny for just a moment and to tell him how thoroughly I had enjoyed his book. A huge grin appeared on his face and I was instantly enveloped in a bear-hug. That was Danny, either suffocating or erasing you. Now, in a small town in the Plains, I had met the other side of a historic coin, a smaller but just as passionate and just as determined Liska. Together they had circled the globe; I felt a circle close as well.

Genesis 6:4 begins, "There were giants in the earth in those days." *There sure were,* I thought as I rolled past what once was the Bigfoot farm the next morning on my way to Omaha. *There sure were.*

A Desert Lottery

Westbound on U.S. 491 to Monticello, Utah

The first thing I must say here is that I wouldn't tell this story if I didn't have photographic proof of its truth. It was a sequence of events of almost reverential stupidity. But I'm told that confession is good for the soul, so let's move along. My soul could use a little buffing.

Fifteen years ago, when I was younger and far more stupid, I was involved in a complex lawsuit that began when a tall man walked down a corridor in Washington's newly remodeled Mayflower Hotel and bumped his head into a lamp fixture that hung from the ceiling. Two weeks later he had a stroke, allegedly losing half of his I.Q. I represented the company, headquartered in Los Angeles, that designed the lamp.

The first move was to meet with the client. I decided to ride my bike out to the West Coast. Why not? It was summertime. I was an experienced Iron Butt kind of guy, having done a 48-state ride in under 11 days the year before. This would be a sort of working vacation. A few days later I was packed up and heading west.

It was hellish that summer. On the second day I rolled through a little town in Tennessee where the bank's thermometer registered 108 degrees. At dawn the following day I pulled over onto the side of the road and got off the bike. The heat was already oppressive. The entirety of Texas lay in front of me. You cannot imagine how big that state is until you've chased it from one end to the other. It didn't cool off until I reached the high desert of Arizona two days later, at which point on U.S. 93 heading north of Wickenburg I began to love motorcycles all over again.

It was a perfect day. My black heart was light. I dote on the desert because it is so empty, vicious, and unforgiving. It seemed as if I could see the ends of the Earth in every direction. I adjusted the throttle's friction screw to keep a steady rate of about 65 mph and pulled a video camera out of the tank bag. *Ready when you are, Mr. DeMille.* I slipped the camera's strap over the back of my right hand, removed the lens cap, steadied the bike with my left hand, and hit the red button to begin recording.

Perhaps this would be an appropriate time to mention that the videotaping technique described above is generally not recommended by motorcycle safety instructors or anyone else. I was steering the bike by mind control. Still, as noted, the high desert is a lonely world where time marches to its own languid pace and nothing much ever happens.

For a while I panned slowly around the horizon. Miles ahead of me was a beautiful escarpment of vermillion cliffs, a common feature of the region. Also ahead of me, but closer, was another car, it too heading north. A tiny ripple of confusion ran up my spine. *Where had he come from? Better yet, how could I be gaining on him so quickly?*

I looked down at the speedometer. It read close to 80. *¿Qué?* I then realized the road was descending slightly. The throttle screw hadn't changed. It had set the motor at a constant rpm, but now I had gained speed — a lot of speed, apparently — because of an almost imperceptible downgrade. I was now just 100 yards behind the car and was cutting that distance by about 10 yards each second. It was definitely time to go back to basics.

I laid the camera on the top of the tank bag and tried to release the back of my right hand from the strap. It was too tight. Had my hand fattened up in the last two minutes? Perhaps I thought of tapping the back brake as an emergency action; I can't recall. Things were happening too rapidly now. I reached across to the throttle with my left hand to try to cut the speed a bit. That's when things really came unglued.

Inadvertently, in attempting to roll the throttle forward and slacken the acceleration, I also pulled back slightly on the right handlebar. That, of course, is the same thing as shoving the left handlebar forward, which, as we all know from motorcycle courses and magazine articles without number, is the definition of countersteering. The result was that even with a trivial amount of tugging from my left hand on the right bar, the bike immediately began to veer to the left into the southbound lane of the highway.

At first I was tremendously relieved, because I now would not rear-end the car ahead of me but would indeed overtake it with a few yards to spare. Then I discovered that a new and even worse problem had arisen: A southbound car had mysteriously appeared on the road and was pointing at my headlight at a closing rate of approximately 150 miles per hour. I had been concentrating so intently on one car that I had utterly overlooked an even worse threat.

As my bike leaned into the lane of oncoming traffic and I saw that in three seconds I would be transformed from Robert E. Higdon, a human, into Robert E. Higdon, a red mist, my only thought was that countersteering had gotten me into this mess and it had better get me out of it.

With my left hand, I pulled on the right bar a little harder. Immediately I swerved left even farther, now onto the shoulder of the southbound lane. I straightened the bike out, my left hand continuing to wrap itself around the throttle in a death grip. I hadn't decreased my speed at all; if anything, I'd gained a little. The video camera — resting on the tank bag, still trapping my right hand, and pointing to the east — continued to roll. What it recorded in the next few seconds was my overtaking a car two lanes to my right and, in the middle of that maneuver, a southbound car coming between us from the opposite direction in a split-second blur. It was a scene straight out of the Keystone Kops.

A few seconds later I managed to swing the bike back into the northbound lane (since by now I was becoming familiar with the lost art of cross-handed countersteering), extricate my hand from the strap, and stuff the camera back in the bag. I don't remember sweating, thinking profound thoughts, or seeing the face of God. I don't remember much of anything except how desperately I wanted to put some distance between me and the car behind me. The idea of his catching up with me at a gas stop was too embarrassing to imagine. What could I say? At one moment the desert had been, as usual, the loneliest place in the universe; a minute later it had turned into a near-suicidal version of a three-ring circus.

The next day my ride west ended at the front door of a four-star hotel in Century City. The doorman, dressed in a Sir Walter Raleigh costume, looked at me, a sunburned rat, contemptuously. Still, the meeting with the client went well, I rode back home without any close calls, and I sold the video camera. Sometimes you make a little money. Sometimes you pay. Occasionally you just break even.

Tucking It Away

Larry Grodsky, the author of "Stayin' Safe," following his good advice

The rain came down. It wasn't the usual late spring rain. It was the kind of deluge I'd once heard described as a cow pissing on a flat rock, something I couldn't quite imagine. Later I saw a cow do it. This rain was like that. Raindrops didn't just smack the pavement; they *bounced off* the pavement.

I staggered into Mama's Diner. Water dripped from equipment I didn't even know I owned. It was one minute before seven in the morning. It isn't my best time of day; I don't function well before about three in the afternoon. I saw a guy sitting in the back of the place. He had to be one of us. He looked chipper.

"Can you believe this crap?" I asked by way of introduction. "We could be in this for the next two days."

He said hello. Rider X was his name, military background, a K75RT owner, therefore cautious, not like George Custer. He's the kind you want to ride with for a couple of days even if you don't know him. He won't get himself into trouble and you won't have to pull him out of it. We'd met, vaguely, somewhere. I can't remember who I met yesterday.

Rider Y came in, shaking water off himself like a dog. He looked even more chipper than X. He peeled off his rainsuit, revealing himself to be a Spandex model. A bicycle racer, he was. Even when I was a teenage life guard I didn't look that good. He rode an FZR or a DMT or a CBQNineThousandLX or something. They're all the same to me. It sat next to my thudding R80G/S in the lot, looking v-e-r-y fast. While we waited for our group leader, we traded small talk and watched the rain knocking holes in the highway.

"I know he's in the area," I said. "He passed me on I-66 west of Gainesville. He was doing about 185 mph on that Ducati."

I was speaking about Larry Grodsky, the safety columnist for *Rider* magazine, who runs a two-day road school in the mountains surrounding the Shenandoah Valley in Virginia. I'd heard about it and had idly thought about signing up one day. Then, two days earlier, he'd called me. There had been a cancellation, he said. Want to come along? And that's why I was in Mama's Diner on the morning of June 10 at the vicious hour of 7:00 a.m., wet and sullen.

There isn't a motorcycle magazine around — with possibly the exception of this holy example of craftsmanship — that I can't go through in about 10 minutes, cover to cover, and then pass a test on reading comprehension. I'll spend a few extra minutes on John Burns or Terry Roorda, but no one speed-reads Grodsky.

He is a cerebral, almost metaphysical, sort of guy. He speaks in parables, favors the passive voice — one of many I'm confident he's conversing with internally as he struggles to carry on a conversation with the human listener standing in front of him — and he often writes the same way. Plowing through Wallace Stevens' incomprehensible verse is a grad-school frolic compared to decrypting Larry Grodsky's prose. You long for a Rosetta stone or a code book or another beer to guide you to enlightenment. When you misstep, you can almost feel your nose being tweaked by the Zen master.

It's worth the effort. He knows what he's doing. Maybe the True Path is achieved only through pain after all. I'd been hoping not.

He showed up just a few minutes late, sodden and disoriented like his students. He put a book of notes on the table, took care of some administrative details, and proceeded to explain the rules. Both days would begin with range exercises, chalk talks, and a review of our progress, if any. On the road we would switch positions on his signal so that we would all have an ample opportunity to trail him and watch him not crash.

We would not ride in staggered formation. He explained why that idea was a crock. In his book he turned to a diagram of four cars, bumper to bumper, hurtling down a two-lane road. Then he drew four staggered motorcyclists coming toward the cars, with bikes No. 1 and No. 3 close to the center line, No. 2 and No. 4 hugging the shoulder. You could almost see one of those imaginary cars coming out to pass.

"Who would you rather be here?" Grodsky asked Socratically. The air chilled. I instantly knew I'd staggered for the last time. Well, on a motorcycle at least.

He finished. The rain stopped. We trooped to an empty parking lot and exercised. After an hour or so we headed off to the south in the general direction of Luray. The pace was brisk but not dangerous. Rider Y, the least experienced, had never been in the mountains.

Grodsky positioned himself on every corner — I'm not saying *most* corners, or the *overwhelming majority* of corners, but *every* corner — to maximize his view around the curve. It looked as if he were late-apexing them all. He said he wasn't. Still, it looked as if we were following a machine riding a machine. It was eerie. Every car that approached from a side road caused him to veer away from it like a vampire from sunlight. When a stack of oncoming cars came at us, he was on the outside edge until they passed.

Wordless examples can be ineradicable. Russ Francis tells a story of being in football camp with the Hall of Fame receiver coach of the Patriots, Raymond Berry, who was, in his prime, Johnny Unitas' favorite target. They stood about two feet apart. Berry tossed a football at Francis. He looked at the ball and tossed it back. Berry grabbed the ball and tucked it away. He stepped back and threw the ball to Francis again. Francis returned it. Berry tucked it away. Every time Francis pitched the ball, Berry would tuck it away.

"I got the message," Francis says. "He never said a word,

but nothing he could have said would have been as effective as that little game of catch we had. If someone would have tossed me a bomb, I'd have probably tucked it away and blown myself up. Even now, if someone spills a drink, I'll catch the ice cube and tuck it away."

Grodsky had warned us not to follow him mechanically. "I'm human," he said. "I make mistakes." I didn't see any. On one curve after another, he would grab it from the outside, peer around the corner, and tuck it away. I got the message.

Up one side of the Blue Ridge and down the other we go. Steam through valleys, take the curves, stop for lunch, and do it again. We follow him. He follows us. We pause. He comments. As the day wears on, I find that he is at last beginning to speak English. He's communicating in a language I can understand. I tuck it away.

We stopped in Natural Bridge that evening. It is billed as one of the seven natural wonders of the world, if the world consists of central Virginia. The day hadn't been long on mileage, but I'd been concentrating and learning and translating the cryptic words of the Pittsburgh oracle. It grinds you down, this stoning with whiffle balls. I was asleep before my eyes closed, tuckered out.

I've been to Reg Pridmore's C.L.A.S.S. and the ERC and read everything I can get my hands on about how to keep a motorcycle upright. You can always learn something new, even if you're a repeat offender in traffic school, and you can never learn enough. Riding a motorcycle is an unforgiving business. Larry Grodsky is trying to make it a little less brutal. He's succeeding, I think. It's been six weeks now and I'm still tucking it away.

[Postscript: Just after sunset on April 8, 2006 Larry was killed when his motorcycle struck a deer on a highway south of Fort Stockton, Texas. A few weeks earlier he had told his girlfriend, Maryann Puglisi, "That's how I'm going to go, it's going to be a deer."]

The Killing Field

PHOTO CREDIT: THE AUTHOR

Bud on the porch rail

We're good friends. We have what is known as "a modern relationship." She sits around the house, eats when she wants to, and generally doesn't bother me. I pay for everything and she sleeps with me. But when she occasionally licks my head in the middle of the night, I think things may have gone too far.

I'm not fond of pointing out character flaws in my bed-mates, but in truth her tongue could sand down a concrete block. To get even I try to pop her with a towel when I come out of the shower, but I always miss. She's faster than I am. She's always been faster, even when she was a kitten.

The theory, I think, about having pets around the house is to teach children about death. It was certainly true in my case. Starting with Mike, a hopeless spaniel, our family witnessed a succession of dogs croak like clockwork. After a while, I didn't even want to think about dogs.

So, in September, 1980, when my wife brought home two kittens, I resigned myself to burying them in a couple of months from some nameless feline killer disease. They were sisters, six weeks old, and I named them Bud and Lou. It's been more than 11 years since that day; the wife has long since departed but Bud and Lou are still here.

Cats are a kind of land-based shark. When they're not sleeping, they're thinking about killing something. One night I was in the guest room, trying to whack a moth that was flitting around the ceiling light. I couldn't come within a foot of hitting it. Out of the corner of my eye, I saw Bud walk by the door. I called to her. She turned and walked into the room.

Then she saw the moth. In the space of a microsecond a hundred million years of phylogeny flickered through her walnut-sized brain.

She hopped onto the bed, crouched, and measured the flight path of the insect. In a blink she was airborne, front legs extended. Before she landed back on the bed, she had snagged the creature out of the air, stuck it in her mouth, and swallowed it. Then she left the room without a backward glance. I was transfixed with the mathematical horror of the event. No ice skater was ever as graceful.

I showed up at Reg Pridmore's final C.L.A.S.S. session of 1991 last November at Willow Springs in the emptiness of the California desert. It was cold and I was scared. Four months earlier in a masterpiece of pilot error I had ridden my K75T to ground in the gravel of a mountain curve in New Mexico. It was the first crash I'd had in 30 years and I didn't want to have another. If Pridmore could teach me how to avoid repeating that awful moment, I'd listen.

The night before a crowd of Iron Butt types had congregated at the only motel in the little town of Rosamond. Mishalof, Kneebone, McQueeney — the usual suspects. Walter Andrews was there, the guy who had taught Fran Crane how to ride faster than the Avenging Horde. Ron Major, the winner of the 1991 Iron Butt Rally. Joe Mandeville, a judge. Big people. Heavy. But they walk like cats.

No worries, they said. Easy does it, they said. You'll love it, really. And be sure to ride on the back of Reggie's bike for a lap or two. I don't know how I got to sleep that night. Bud can sleep 20 hours a day.

I am with the B group, as opposed to the A team, even though neither is my blood type. B is for rookies, geeks, creampuffs; A is racers, wannabes, people who believe in gyroscopes. Our group stands by turn eight and watches the A riders come by at 80 on an early lap. They head into the final turn, a descending radius corner that looks vicious even from a distance. In a while they're back, but now they're hunkered down, doing 100-plus. The ground throbs, the trailing wind rips at everything not nailed down, and only a deathly silence remains. *My God*, I think, *they've unleashed the Dogs of War.*

The A guys retire to the classroom. We B people do a few laps, trying to memorize The Line, and no one is moving more slowly than am I. In the middle of the straight, an FZR comes up on me, shifts, and rockets past with a hellish noise. I loop and loop, staring at the corners, watching the Gold Wing pass me, waiting for the Zen master to tweak my nose and deliver enlightenment, satori, The Way. It isn't coming. I roll into the pit.

Pridmore isn't doing rides until mid-afternoon and I need an answer to this barren place now. "Take me for a ride, please," I ask his son, Jason. "I don't know what I'm supposed to do." He smiles and gets his helmet. He has a New Wave haircut that resembles Bud's tail when she's surprised by a squirrel in the back yard.

I sit on the rear, leaning forward with my fingertips pressing against the tank of the K100RS. This isn't how I'd imagined it would be. I want to hold onto him, tightly. But this isn't holding on. This is *praying*. We're not out of the pit before I'm having misgivings on a cosmic scale. And then it gets worse in a hurry.

The bike launches itself toward turn two, a long, arcing right-hander. Pridmore's style is to cut toward the inside of every corner, to take away the ability of a trailing bike to pass, but there are no bikes out here that will pass him today or would even want to try. When it dawns on me that he really is going to slam into that turn at some godless speed, I try to suppress a moan. A moment later he has the machine heeled over to the right at an angle that shakes me to my core. *This is going to hurt like hell*, I think. *But I'll be unconscious then and won't give a damn anymore.*

And with that realization a sublime peace envelopes me, as if my nerve endings had been coated with morphine. We exit the turn still alive, take turn three to the inside (as usual), become almost airborne at turn four, shriek downhill to the 90-degree left-hander (inside), and cover the hundreds of yards of back straight in less time than it takes me to recite the Apostle's Creed. He doesn't come off on pit road, but takes another lap. By now my spirit is two hundred yards above the bike, circling the track casually like a bird, watching my corporeal form on the back of a red bike blur through time and space without sorrow, toil, or care. And then it is over.

No one passed me the rest of the day. In the late afternoon the fellow on the Wing told me how well he thought I'd been riding. "If you wouldn't mind," I replied, "would you please tell that to the lady over there?" When I last saw him, he was heading in Fran Crane's direction.

Recently I saw a PBS program about hyenas. A pack of them was harrying a wounded lioness. I started to become excited about the essential injustice of life. Then Bud came down the stairs. "Come here, my man. You ought to see this." She jumped up on my lap.

A male lion emerges from the bush, trotting toward the camera, with murder on his mind. Picking up the scent of one of the hyenas, he breaks into attack mode and begins boring down on the filthy, dog-like thing. The hyena jigs left and right, but the lion closes remorselessly. He sweeps a paw out, barely misses, then tracks the prey on an extreme hard right. I cannot understand why the lion doesn't fall at that lean angle.

"Just like Pridmore in turn two, Bud. It's over." The lion flicks out another paw and the hyena falls. "*Yes!*" I cry exultantly. "*Yes!*"

Bud looks up at me. I'm still smiling. Maybe she is too. It's hard to tell.

Tchebycheff and Me

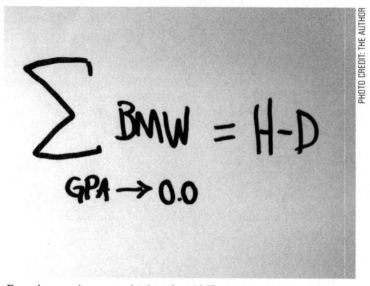

Formula on a classroom whiteboard at AMI

First, it gets cold. Then the snow comes, more than two feet. Mayor-for-Life Marion Barry, neutered by Prozac, mumbles incoherently that all streets in the District of Columbia will be plowed within 48 hours. The city promptly grinds to an apocalyptic halt for two weeks. Crime rates drop because the Jamaican drug gangs are snowbound.

Warm rains come to pound the area and melt mountains of snow. The Potomac overflows, wiping out the sewage-treatment plant and offering to submerge the lobby of the garish Kennedy Center in a foot of contaminated mud.

Then temperatures plummet again. Blocks of barn-sized ice hammer into bridge pilings, shutting some escape routes to Virginia. Even if I could ride, I know that the bike's O-rings are rigid from weeks in an unheated garage. Merely to crank up the machine invites a fireball. Ask the engineers at Morton Thiokol.

I stare out the kitchen window at a scene from *Dr. Zhivago*. Frogs, locusts, and other Biblical precipitation cannot be far off. By the end of the fourth week of January I have ridden a total of two (2) miles. They were ugly miles, too. I returned home, twitching with cold, and sent a message to a moto computer board: "As short as it was, this was one of the worst rides I've ever taken."

And I thought, "How bad was it really?" On a scale of nil to 10, was it a zero? No, a ride worth a zero would end with someone drawing a chalk outline around my body. How about a five? Never. A middling score like that should mean that at least part of the ride was enjoyable. Three? As I considered that mark, my fingers were still white from frostbite. It couldn't even be a crummy three. Maybe two.

Being digitally disposed and anal-retentive at heart (to mix just three anatomical metaphors), I wanted to find an objective method of rating a day's ride. What makes a good ride, I knew intuitively, is the absence of pain. So I needed a rogue's gallery of pain producers to factor into an equation.

As luck would have it, at that very moment President Bubba was delivering his Stasis of the Union address. I stared at the array of liars, misfits, and bed-wetting mutants in the House chamber. "Whores," I mumbled vacantly.

Whores? That was it! The perfect acronym to describe the elements of a motorcycle ride: **W**ind (direction and velocity); **H**eat (or its more vicious opposite); **O**neness with the universe (quantifying a state of mind); **R**oad (traction and condition); **E**lements (fog, rain, sleet, snow, hail, tidal waves, atomic attack, and frogs); and **S**cenery (the Cross-Bronx Expressway being the point below which further discussion is pointless).

With the necessary BBs now in hand, all that remained was to stack them in a pristinely arithmetic shape. The novice might presume that since there are six WHORES, each should logically be worth 1.6666667 points for an Olympian 10 in the aggregate.

But the categories clearly are not of equal misery. Atrocious scenery is not as debilitating as a 40-mph crosswind. Temperatures of 8 degrees cannot gut a ride as quickly as ice on a cliff-hanger mountain road. The variables had to be weighted somehow.

A yet more imposing problem loomed. Gauging the Scenery factor isn't hard. Give the Cross-Bronx a zero and Utah Route 95 the max. The same for Oneness: the better your mood, the higher your score.

And not all the categories are linear. A headwind isn't as bad as a crosswind and neither is as good as a ripping tailwind. In such a case a quadratic equation is needed, maybe something even tougher. The Heat factor begs for a Gaussian distribution, kurtotically skewed to whichever end of the temperature scale you prefer. So I dragged out the mothballed statistics books and began to stare at the ancient formulas.

Years ago I understood that trying to master statistics without the benefit of calculus was a fool's errand. I had forgotten that simple rule. After spending a few days with turgid tomes of statistical analysis, a smoking calculator, and a half-ream of shredded notes, I realized I'd stumbled into a one-way tunnel.

The end came with a footnote that explained the Tchebycheff Inequality. Without a trace of humor it said that within a range of +/- T standard deviations "there will be contained not less than 1-(1/T2) proportion of the observations." After glaring at that for a few minutes, I knew that one day I might give a big damn what "T" was. This was hopeless.

I slumped back, for some reason thinking of Edgar Allen Poe's essay explaining how he hit upon "Nevermore" as the leitmotif for *The Raven*. He claimed it was a process of near mathematical deduction. Grad students in English have been chuckling about that for the last hundred years. As I chuckled, suddenly The Answer appeared.

The key is Oneness. It overwhelms the other variables. If your mood is invincible, nothing else much matters, not potholes or hurricanes or the New Jersey Turnpike. And while trying to traverse the Cross-Bronx is about as bad as it gets, death is arguably worse. If someone is notifying your next of kin at day's end, that plainly should cancel everything else.

The rest was easy. The worst case in each category is zero. Maximum values vary because, as noted, they are of unequal weight: Wind = 3; Heat = 4; Oneness = 5; Road = 10; Elements = 6; and Scenery = 2;

Now gently insert everything into this formula:

$$FU = 2 * \sqrt[3]{M * (W + H + R + E + S)}$$

The answer is expressed in FUs, or fun units. To assist our arithmetically challenged readers, M (for mood) is substituted for the O in Oneness, lest any reader mistakenly insert zero into the equation and wonder why recent rides have suddenly become so consistently depressing.

Advanced students will see that with all variables maxed out, FU = 10. The worst possible score is zero. That occurs only when oneness (M) equals zip. Midpoint scores in each category yield 6.3 FUs, which isn't that bad when you recall how grim a bike ride truly can be.

Take an example. The wind is gusty from the rear-quarter (2.4) and the temperature is 10 degrees lower than you'd like (3.0). The road was fine until that section of gravel (7.7). The fog lifted (5.3), but you're adrift on I-95 (0.6). You've ridden hard because your girlfriend might be in her dominatrix mood if you can arrive before she starts drinking. Your Oneness is a cautious but optimistic 3.6.

Plug and crank: Add up the W, H, R, E, and S and multiply the sum by Oneness. Grab its cube root. Multiply that by two to get 8.2. QED.

I don't know about you, but I'll take an 8.2 any day, especially one that ends with Tiffany and her leather nightie. I just hope she's not already into the second six-pack.

[Postscript: The formula in the photograph accompanying the story appeared on a classroom whiteboard one day in the fall of 1994 when I was attending the American Motorcycle Institute, a trade school for bike mechanics. In a parody of a calculus formula it suggests that as a student's grade-point average deteriorates, the more likely he will be to wind up working on Harleys. Since I was in the BMW program at the school, I thought it was a pretty good joke. Could it be any more nonsensical than using a quadratic equation to determine the quality of a day's ride?]

RIDER – DECEMBER 2004

Slogging Through Siberia

Moscow's Red Square

The intersection of all our pains came in Magdagachi. Mike was so sick he couldn't eat. The only solid thing that had emerged from Steve in the past week was some phlegm from his dust-caked lungs. John's bike threatened daily to crack into fore and aft sections. And I, squatting precariously over a fetid hole in the floor at half past three in the morning with earplugs stuffed in my nose, was trying to figure out a way to kill myself and make it look like an accident.

It hadn't started like this. A trip across Russia from west to east that Iron Butt Association president Mike Kneebone and I began in the summer of 2002 ended disastrously when my bike, a well-prepped but ancient BMW dual-sport R80G/S, came apart at the seams before we'd reached Moscow. We retreated to Europe, as had Napoleon and Hitler before us, vowing to return.

We learned a few things from that abortive ride: 1) Take new, identical bikes; 2) Find a traveling companion who spoke Russian; and 3) Get the hard part out of the way first by riding east to west.

We resolved Issue No. 1, the bikes, by opting for 2003 Honda Nighthawks, machines so maintenance-free that they oil themselves at night while you're in the bar knocking back a vodka gimlet. Sure, they're street bikes and worthless on mud and sand, but we were going to be on pavement the entire way. What about that 1,500-mile stretch of impassable swamp in eastern Siberia between Khabarovsk and Chita, you might ask? No worries, because we'll stick the bikes on a train, slip ourselves into a first-class sleeper, and spend our waking hours playing backgammon with the other rich passengers in the club car.

Issues No. 2 and No. 3, locating both a translator-rider and the starting point for the journey, were solved with one stroke. Through mutual friends we found John Sartorius. He spoke Russian fluently, was a good mechanic, had done some amateur racing, and (best of all) was eager to do a big ride across Mother Russia. Everyone's schedules, concepts, goals, and Top Ten lists meshed with eerie precision.

John planned to take his '91 R100GS BMW. Mike and I would buy the Nighthawks at Sunnyside Motorcycle Company near Yakima, Washington, in the fall of 2003, have them outfitted and broken in by Iron Butt Association legend Dale Wilson, trucked to the shipper in Seattle, and freighted by sea to Sakhalin. We all would meet on July 1, 2004, spend July 2 packing the bikes and confessing our sins, and start the ride to Moscow — 7,000 miles to the west — on July 3. An overnight ferry to the mainland would be followed with a day's jaunt to Khabarovsk. There, because the road west basically didn't exist except between occasional towns, we'd put the bikes on the train for three days to Chita, the capital of eastern Siberia. From there it was a paved road all the way to the Atlantic Ocean. That was the plan, set in stone.

The first crack in the stone came when Russian President Vladimir Putin announced in the spring of 2004 — when our Nighthawks were on the container ship bound for Russia — that the road linking Vladivostok in the east with St. Petersburg in the west was now open. Engineers had been working on that highway for more than 35 years. It was now officially the longest road on Earth. And if the road traversing the swamp between Khabarovsk and Chita was actually open, wouldn't we be obliged at least to try it?

Another stone crack occurred when Steve Attwood, an Englishman who won the 1993 Iron Butt Rally, heard about our proposed exploit and expressed a desire to come along. Mike and I have soft spots in our hearts for the man. Self-effacing to the point where he disappears, Steve rides a bike the way Fred Astaire danced: You can see what he's doing, but you don't know how he does it.

"We're starting in Sakhalin," I said. "How would you get your bike there from England?"

"Ride it," he said.

I considered that for a moment. He proposed to travel almost halfway around the

Mike Kneebone after another hard day on the road in Siberia

world to meet us at the start. For him there would be no plane, no train, nor magic carpet. He would take a single-cylinder KTM 640, the street version of the bike that has won recent Paris-Dakar rallies. Though he'd be unable to speak five words in any of the local languages or read the Cyrillic alphabet, he promised to hook up with us 10 time zones east of his home, rest for a few days, and ride 10,000 miles back the way he had come. I shuddered at the thought.

So at the appointed time the four of us met on a cold island in the western Pacific. It was drizzling and 49 degrees as we parked our bikes on the Pacific shore for the obligatory photo op. Cheese. Snap. Let's go. Fifty miles away was the overnight ferry that would carry us from Sakhalin to Vanino, Russia's

Steve Attwood

mainland port. Awaiting us was the world's longest highway. It wasn't a toll road, but it would take one anyway.

The next morning we docked four hours late, guaranteeing that we wouldn't arrive in Khabarovsk until after midnight. That violates Rule No. 1 of motorcycle travel in foreign countries: Never ride at night. We cleared customs, filled the tanks, and 10 minutes later were sitting on one of the worst dirt roads I have ever seen. Steve had traveled over this stretch the week before. No one had better information about conditions in eastern Russia than we did, but the information was hardly comforting.

"The next 200 miles will be a preview of everything you'll see from here to Moscow," Steve said darkly. "Bad dirt, worse pavement, washouts, rocks, gravel, mud, sand, dust, and road works that you really won't believe."

I stared at the grim-looking road before me and shook my head. If the moon had air, my companions could ride through its craters with a smile. Not me. I'm a street guy, old enough to be their father, and more comfortable receiving Social Security checks than instructions on how to plow through sand. Damn. I stabbed the bike into first gear and moved forward. Turning around was not an option.

We staggered into the Versailles Hotel in Khabarovsk at half past one in the morning, more than 13 hours and 400 miles after we'd left Vanino. When we'd dreamed up this journey months earlier, I hadn't planned on having a single day as draining as the one I'd just had. Now it looked as if I had a string of them yet to face. I asked to meet with everyone the next morning for a strategy conference.

"Here are the choices," I said when we gathered for breakfast. "We can put the bikes on the train to Chita right now or we can try to ride there. I'd like to see how the Trans-Siberian Railway works. Would anyone else?" No one spoke. The original plan was circling the drain.

I looked at Steve. "I know that it's theoretically possible to ride between here and Chita because you've done it within the last two weeks. Has anyone else on a bike made it through?"

"Two Finnish riders," he replied. "One of them broke a shock spring. It took them 10 days to do the 1,500 miles." I tried to absorb that knowledge. What kind of road can break a shock *spring?*

"Has anyone not made it?" I asked.

"A Japanese guy crashed two days west of here and had to be carried out. A Frenchman coming from Chita turned back after a day and put the bike on the train. I haven't heard of anyone else trying it."

And he would have heard. That I knew. You'd think in an area as unimaginably vast as Siberia — almost twice the size of the continental U.S. with one-tenth the population density — that verifiable information would be non-existent. But there's essentially only one road and the word spreads from traveler to traveler in both directions. Every globe-trotting biker pays attention to the drums. They are more reliable than the *International Herald Tribune*.

"It took you three-and-a-half days from Chita to here. Hell, man, it could take me a *week*. That's assuming I can make it at all. Are you guys ready for that possibility?"

They all nodded.

I tried desperately to wrap my brain around what lay before us. Mike, the ultimate wing man, would stick with me no matter what I did. But nothing was going to dissuade John and Steve from attacking that road. When he left England, Steve worried that riding across Russia and back wouldn't be enough of a challenge. To give some real credibility to the ride, he thought he might have to detour into Mongolia or China. But by the time he had reached Sakhalin, he had decided that traveling Russia's longest road in both directions was definitely "enough."

In the end it boiled down to this: 1) There was a road to the west that could be traversed because three riders had already done it; and 2) If I put my bike on the train, I'd almost certainly lose permanent contact with John, our translator. As much as I longed for the comfort and security of the railway, I recoiled at the thought of losing John even more. Russian is a difficult language. No one we were likely to meet would be able to speak two words of English. No, I couldn't lose John.

"Let's do it," I said.

In mid-afternoon we saw evidence of a dirt road from two miles away. A brown cloud hung in the air like a permanent feature of the landscape. Recent construction was apparent. The only vehicles around, apart from construction equipment or an occasional long-haul truck, were used Japanese cars that had been imported through Vladivostok for resale in Siberia's larger cities. Such trafficking was illegal — like the GPS receivers we carried — but no one seemed to care.

John Sartorius

After 20 miles, we recovered pavement, only to bounce back into the dirt a few miles later. The pattern would repeat itself for the next two days. Each mile west seemed to be imperceptibly a little harder than the last. We called it a day in the small town of Obluche by early evening, 230 miles west of Khabarovsk.

Tourist accommodations in the Russian Far East are practically non-existent. Most towns of any consequence will have a hotel that was built during the Soviet era, but you won't confuse it with a Motel 6. Your room is always on the top floor. It will be relatively clean, but there may be no electricity. The bathroom and shower are down the hall, but there probably won't be any hot water. After a few nights of this sort of

Spartan life, you might think that you'd be better off camping in the woods.

If you thought that, you'd be wrong. Much of eastern Siberia is a primordial swamp. That kind of terrain, combined with a short summer, produces ravenous mosquitoes and other insects. None of us had ever seen anything quite like it. You can endure a cold shower, but I don't know anyone who can endure a horsefly cloud.

The wetland aspect of the region is another reason it has been so difficult to complete the Siberian section of the highway. Seemingly interminable construction puts one layer of gravel on top of an older crushed layer. This can continue until the surface of the roadbed rises to treetop level. Until the new gravel has been dispersed by traffic, bike travel can be an exercise in sliding along in first gear, eating dust kicked up by trucks lumbering by in both directions.

The rain subdued the dust the next day, but created its own problems. Potholes filled with water that was the color of the road surface. Even if you could see what was coming, you wouldn't miss them all. I limped along, going so slowly at times that bugs would overtake me, fly up under the face shield, and bite me on the nose. At one point a passenger in a passing car rolled down his window and aimed a camera at me. That was when I began to realize I was engaged in a unique adventure.

By noon the relentless pounding from road washouts had broken saddlebag racks on both Steve's bike and mine. John found a welding shop in the town of Savintsk, where we became instant celebrities. Four mechanics began to pull the bikes apart as more than a score of people showed up to observe us. They asked for our autographs. Tape recorders and video cameras appeared. We would be seen on the evening television news throughout the province. It was a mobile zoo, and we were the alien motorcyclists who inhabited it.

I'd grown up fearing that Russians at any moment were preparing to lob a hydrogen bomb through the window of my social studies classroom at Grant Junior High School. "Duck and cover," Miss Kelley had told us. Behind that iron curtain were the most evil sons of bitches the world had ever known. Miss Kelley taught me to view them with a Biblical kind of suspicion, and I learned that lesson well.

Now, on a hot, wet afternoon in a small town in eastern Siberia, the descendants of the people who had given me so many childhood nightmares were taking us to a late lunch, spending almost three hours fixing our broken machines, and inviting us wholesale into their lives with genuine delight. The total bill for the repair of both bikes was about $25. They seemed almost offended when we pressed them fruitlessly to accept more. The Cold War, at least for me, was indeed over and done with.

We came into Belogorsk at dusk, the end of another 12-hour day with not much progress (220 miles). The rain, hard roads, and delays for repairs had cost us again. We didn't know it, but it would only get worse.

Weather windows in Siberia are narrow and the riding season laughably short. If you try to cross the countryside in May, as the Finns did, you'll run into snow. In June it will freeze at night but it might not snow. July will bring out the flies, afternoon thunderstorms, and 95-degree heat. In August it starts snowing again.

The winter defies description. Our route took us a little south of some of the lowest temperatures ever recorded outside Antarctica. Fifty below zero — steel shatters in such cold — is not uncommon in the area. A drunk will stagger out of a bar, fall down in a stupor, and be quickly covered up by a snowfall. The following May, as the ice slowly melts, the snow bank begins to reveal an upraised frozen arm or leg. The Russians call these apparitions *podsnezhniki*, spring flowers.

The first three days had been rough. On the fourth day, things turned seriously ugly. We had stopped for gas after noon, having come off a stretch of pavement that was hopeless even by Siberian standards. I looked at Mike and tried to smile.

"As bad as that was," I said, "it still beats the dirt." I

John Sartorius leading the author and Steve Attwood through endless Siberia

should have shut up. It was the last paved road we would see for the next 900 miles.

Almost immediately the highway deteriorated into deep sand and broken rocks. Twice Mike and I stopped to confirm that this really was the road to Magdagachi. For more than 15 miles we picked our way through the debris. At our next gas stop, Mike snapped that it hadn't been so much a construction zone as a war zone.

Half an hour later, on the outskirts of a town, my bike suddenly low-sided in a foot of sand. The Nighthawk and I weren't hurt — the sand was so deep it had acted almost as a cushion — but what little self-confidence I'd had was now gone with the wind.

Magdagachi was a bad place. It was old, ugly, and hot. Soviet fingerprints were everywhere. Stalin loved cottonwood trees, so every town in Russia years ago had planted thousands of them to please the tyrant. In Magdagachi that evening, the airborne pollen was so thick it looked almost as if it were snowing.

Our collective mood was grim. Mike, too woozy to come to dinner, slept. John, Steve, and I looked for a restaurant. We were all wearing T-shirts. The waiter at The Oasis tried to turn us away because we weren't suitably dressed. We'd had too hard a day for this kind of crap. John began to argue with him so noisily that the owner came to the door. Two minutes later we were at a table with a round of Baltika beer in front of us. We were the restaurant's only customers.

"That's typical of the way things used to be," John said. "It's the Soviet mindset. If the waiter can dream up a reason to keep us out, then he won't have to do any work. Things are changing, but it will take some time."

I sucked on the beer morosely. Stories of the old days in the workers' paradise were of some historical interest, but my focus was more on how I was going to get my sagging butt to the paved highway in Chita before I did any further damage to the bike or, worse, to myself.

"How do you guys do this?" I asked. "You can go 60 mph on these crappy roads. I'm lucky if I can do 25."

They looked at each other blankly. It was so obvious to them, yet so mysterious to me.

"The bike talks to me," Steve said finally. "I can feel it through the pegs and the bars. It's telling me what it's going to do. I respond to that."

"I know exactly what you mean," I said, taking another swig of Baltika. "My bike talks to me too. It says, *You're so pathetic and incompetent that I'm going to throw your wrinkled ass into a ditch the first chance I get.* I've been hoping it would say something a little more pleasant, but so far that's all I've been hearing."

"We'll take some more air out of your tires tomorrow," Steve said. "That will help."

"I don't know why," I snarled. "It can't get any worse than it was today."

"Bob, it gets *much* worse than this. We haven't gotten to the road works yet."

As tired as I was, I couldn't sleep that night. Before Magdagachi, I was concerned; now I was becoming frightened. Falling in the sand can bruise your hip or elbow. Falling on a rock may break an arm or leg. Then what? Dialing 911 won't work in Siberia. We were at the epicenter of absolutely nowhere. There is no medevac helicopter, no ambulance, no taxi. Maybe a truck can bounce you 500 miles to a dispensary, but assuming you live through the ride, there won't be an X-ray machine or medicine. This was insane.

When Mike woke up, I told him I was going to put the bike on the train.

"John can handle the details at the station," I said. "We can all meet up at the best hotel in Chita in a few days. How about that?"

Mike shook his head slowly. "There might not be a train through here for a week."

He was right. I sagged back against the wall. *Bob, it gets much worse than this.*

Did it ever. We hit the construction zone outside of Skorovodino in the late afternoon. What had been a wretched but at least identifiable road didn't just stop — it disintegrated into a sea of rocks the size of footballs. I looked around abjectly. If Dante could have seen this, he might have revised his idea of what the inferno really looked like. A man sitting on an enormous bulldozer in the distance pointed a finger toward the northwest. Steve pulled up next to me and motioned for me to follow. We began to tiptoe the bikes through the slag pile. It took an hour to travel the next three miles.

Not long after that we stopped at a machine shop to fabricate a ¾-inch bolt that held John's left saddlebag to the subframe. Vibration had cracked it in half. As Mike and Steve were disassembling the bike, one of the shop's welders said to John, "I've never been to Germany, but I've heard that the roads are so smooth there that you can read a book as you drive your car." I dimly recalled roads like that, but I hadn't seen any for a while.

That night John found a place for us in a worker's dormitory in Yerofey Pavlovich, a small town that apparently owed its existence to the railroad. We hiked 150 yards to the town's communal shower, which was heated by a coal-fed boiler two stories high. The dust had become an integral part of us. We were perpetually filthy. Zippers had stopped working. Any break in the skin produced an infection. So we scrubbed away, for whatever trivial good it might do.

In Iron Butt Association circles a 1,000-mile day is where the conversation starts. Anything less than that isn't worth discussing. By the start of our *fifth* day in Siberia, we had not ridden a total of 1,000 miles, and pavement was still almost 500 miles to the west. I kept hoping that conditions would improve, but they methodically got worse. Between the loose gravel where new road construction was occurring and the dreadful, corrugated cart paths that masqueraded as the old road, making any sort of reasonable speed was impossible for me. Because I was so much slower than the others, I would keep riding when they took tea breaks in the morning or afternoon. If I'd stopped with them, we might be in Siberia yet.

Long ago the road had ground down any romantic notions I might have harbored about this ride. No more did I care about seeing the house near Yekaterinburg where the Bolsheviks mowed down the czar and his family like summer wheat. Forget finding Dr. Zhivago's dacha at Varykino. Even if it existed, it would probably be covered in dust and mosquitoes. No. Get home in one piece. That's all I cared about.

Late in the morning John rode back to us from a scouting foray with some disquieting news. He had been told that an oil refinery in the province had ceased production. Nothing but 80-octane fuel would be available in a radius of 300 miles during the next several weeks. I asked Mike if the poor

Nighthawks could run on gruel like that. He thought so, if we avoided lugging the engines.

It was at that point, I think, that I slowly leaned back on the seat and surrendered. For more days than I could remember I had hated what that horrendous road had done to the battered motorcycle and even more what it had done to me. I had been furious at Russia for . . . well, being Russia. And Russia didn't care whether I was irritated or not. Russia is simply too big to care about anything. If I'd had a white flag, I'd have waved it.

It would be the longest day of all — 14 hours, no breakdowns, but no better than a pathetic 17 mph average, either. We spent the night on bunk beds in a road-construction camp trailer that night, treated like visiting royalty by the crew. They poured beer and vodka into us, rolled out the food, fired up the boiler for a sauna, and kept us up until two in the morning. When we wearily left the next morning to face the last day of dirt before Chita, John said, "Russian hospitality can kill you."

At five minutes before five that afternoon the pavement reappeared like a beautiful ribbon. I got off the bike, lay on my belly, and kissed the asphalt. That last day had been as exhausting as all the others, this time with more than 100 miles of sand that had sunk me into first gear for more than an hour. The Nighthawk's air filter was so clotted with dirt that, until we banged it on the pavement to clean it out, the weary bike wouldn't pull more than 4,200 rpm without choking to death.

There is an unforgettable scene in the movie *The Perfect Storm* where George Clooney, in the wheelhouse of a small fishing boat, stares at a dark, roiling sea. A break in the clouds throws sunlight onto his face for a moment. His first mate thinks they have might have a chance to survive. But shadows quickly darken Clooney's face and he shakes his head almost imperceptibly. "It's not going to let us out," he says with the resignation of a man who can count the minutes remaining in his life on the fingers of one hand.

I had never wanted to be on that vile road out of Khabarovsk. Once I was on it, I wondered sometimes if it would ever let me out. Somehow it did. I'm not sure why. Maybe my surrender helped. But a week after landing on the mainland of Russia we arrived in Chita, with its gorgeous Hotel Panama City, telephones, television, hot water, and bowling alley. When we thought about having a Chinese dinner that evening, Mike suggested that we skip

Michel Marek, on the road in the middle of Siberia

the imitators and go straight to the source. He had a point. China itself was 290 miles to the southeast. Mongolia was even closer.

But, to paraphrase Robert Frost, we had promises to keep and miles to go before we'd be even halfway through Siberia. Ahead of us lay Ulan-Ude, a city famous for harboring both the world's largest sculpture of Lenin's head, and the lineal descendants of Genghis Khan. The day after that we would reach the shores of Lake Baikal, which holds one-fifth of the Earth's fresh water. Beyond there we would come into the steppes of central Asia, 2,000 miles of plain whose elevation never rises above 600 feet until you bump into the Ural mountains. Two days farther west was Moscow. The distances seemed almost intergalactic.

We knew from other travelers that the paved roads would be no picnic. We'd find manholes with no manhole covers, traffic lights with no light bulbs, and, with no parents in sight, toddlers running into the middle of traffic. Rather than design complex switchbacks, highway engineers routinely plow straight up a 12-percent grade, causing overloaded trucks to bog on the ascent, blanketing the highway with diesel smoke, and to lose their brakes on the way down. Throw into that mix the most aggressive drivers you can imagine and for a moment you might look back nostalgically to the days when you were in the mountains of eastern Siberia, dodging a pothole on a rotted road or sliding through a new layer of gravel.

In Moscow John had arranged for us to stay with some friends of his from the old days. One night Steve and I sat at a kitchen table, separated by a bottle of high-test vodka, after the others had retired. He had changed the oil on his KTM that morning, discovering particles of a bearing that was grinding itself to bits. He wouldn't be riding with us to the Ukraine. Indeed, he would be lucky to make it to Finland, where his towing insurance could kick in after the motor digested itself. Curiously, his mood was good. He wondered why mine wasn't.

"You've done it, Bob," he said. "Take credit for it."

"Nah," I said. "I was in a fire. I jumped out of the building, that's all. You don't get credit for that."

"I love it here," he said. "I can't wait to come back."

I could see where this was going. As a recovering lawyer, I felt an obligation to give my friend some free advice.

"When I was a kid," I recalled, "I lived for a while in Japan. One summer I climbed Mt. Fujiyama. Our maid was proud of me. She said that every good Japanese climbs Fuji at least once. Suppose I did it again, I asked her. That would be even better, Sumiko-san agreed. Climbing Fuji twice is a sign of exceptional devotion."

I paused, took a hit of vodka, and stared across the table.

"I never made the second climb," I told Steve. "But you have. You've crossed Russia twice. That's enough."

"What's wrong with a third try?" he wondered.

"I asked Sumiko about that. She said that anyone who climbs Fuji three times is a fool."

We all eventually reached the shores of the Atlantic by separate routes and ritualistically dipped our front tires in the surf. My Nighthawk returned by air cargo from Europe to Dulles airport. I then rode it from Virginia to Seattle, arriving at the shipper's offices where the bike had originally been put on the container vessel months earlier. On a foggy September 20, 2004, morning, Jeff Holt, the agent who had arranged for the transport of our bikes to Russia, took a photograph of the Honda and me in front of his office on the south side of Seattle. I had ridden around the world in 80 days.

Before I cranked up the Nighthawk for the ride back to the East Coast, I thought about Russia again for a moment. It had been a tough ride, no doubt. Still, there was so much I hadn't seen, detours to China and Mongolia I hadn't taken, centuries of history I had left unexplored. Could I really walk away from that massive country, a land that had conquered every invader who had foolishly stepped across its borders? Walk away without a second look? Ah, sure I could.

But before I'd ridden 10 miles, I already knew that one day I would have to go back. Russia had conquered me too.

The Visitor

PHOTO CREDIT: CHUCK WEST

Fran Crane

Antoine de St. Exupéry's novella, *The Little Prince*, is usually found in the children's section of bookstores. Like most good children's stories, of course, the tale of the diminutive visitor from asteroid B612 is really an allegory for adults. It is a story about life and death and letting go.

St. Exupéry knew those subjects firsthand. He had been one of the first French aviators, had flown mail routes through the Andes in the 1930s, and had crashed in the Sahara during an air race from Paris to Saigon. He seemed able to survive anything. But on a routine reconnaissance flight in northern France during World War II, he disappeared, as they say, without a trace.

I once knew a woman from St. Exupéry's asteroid B612. She was a motorcyclist, a very fast and efficient motorcyclist, and she could stay on her bike for so long that it seemed as if she and the machine had bonded together. One day we rode together for about 50 yards. That's when I figured out that she wasn't from around here.

It was at a C.L.A.S.S. session at the Willow Springs race track. I had jumped into the sub-novice "B" group and was plowing around the course on my K75 at speeds that were slow even by sub-novice standards. But I was learning. Even the downhill, off-camber, left-hand corner that had been designed by the devil himself was succumbing to my iron will.

By the middle of the day, I was hammering through there at speeds well in excess of 18 mph. As I approached the corner for perhaps the 30th time, I slung the bike over to a frightening angle of maybe 10 degrees off vertical, geared down, cranked up the throttle to 2,500 rpm, clamped both hands on the grips, and hung on for dear life. At that moment my eyes were blurred, naturally, but I still could see a rider coming around the outside of that hellish corner at an unbelievable speed, pointing at me with a left thumb up in the air and grinning. In a couple of moments the bike and rider had disappeared, as they say, without a trace.

I am not easily impressed, but that particular feat stepped me back so much that I came into the pits and made an inquiry about the little guy in the gray leathers on the K-bike. I was told that the little guy was Fran Crane and that she was one of the C.LA.S.S. instructors.

That was the only time I ever saw her ride, those 50 yards. It was enough. It told me that she wasn't from around here. But, hell, everybody knew that.

If it was a motorcycle endurance competition, at one time or another Fran held the record. The quickest time touching each of the 48 states? In 1988 she and Mike Kneebone did it in 6.6 days, shattering the old record, held by me, by more than four days and establishing a new one that would stand for 10 years. Forty-eight hours later, she went back home across the U.S. in record time from New York to San Francisco. When the American Motorcyclist Association's museum did a tribute to women in motorcycling some years ago, the rider from asteroid B612 was a significant part of the exhibition.

Now she has gone, the target of a perverse concatenation of bad luck and worse luck. With 96 percent of the Iron Butt Rally behind her and only minutes after filling the bike's tank, she mysteriously lost control of the motorcycle on an interstate highway. A helmet that should not fail failed, but she was otherwise injured only slightly. She was taken to a modern, reputable hospital suffering from nothing more critical than a concussion. She began to recover, but then was mistakenly administered a drug that ended her life. At any point the fracture of a single link in that inexorable chain of circumstances would today have Fran alive and well. But nothing intervened. When people speak of cruel fate, this is what they mean.

It is neither surprising nor ironic to me that the airplane which gave St. Exupéry's life such meaning and expression was also the instrument of his death. Thus it is with Fran and her motorcycle. No machines that toy with gravity the way airplanes and motorcycles do will ever be safe. Those who love to fly them or ride them appreciate that risk and accept it for what it is worth. You hope your bet won't be called; but you know that if you fly or ride long enough and fast enough, it likely will be. When that happens, sadness reigns. It is inevitable.

St. Exupéry left us his beautiful words and images; Fran has left us her beautiful grace, skill, and spirit. We cannot ask any more of them than that. We are lucky to have known these magnificent people at all, however tangentially and however briefly. In their deaths they have taught us about life.

Along the lonely roads of Nevada at night, you simply cannot believe the light show that the heavens produce. The stars literally are without number. They wink and sputter and rip across the sky joyously. You can almost hear them laughing. There are comets and meteors and space junk, constellations and nebulae and galaxies, and worlds without end.

There are asteroids up there, too. Look for the one called B612. Any child can point it out to you. That one's my favorite. I once knew a person from there.

ON THE LEVEL - OCTOBER 1996

The Operating Room

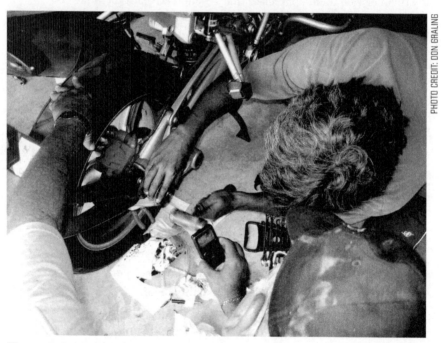

PHOTO CREDIT: DON GRALING

The surgical team at work

On the last Thursday of most months, two dozen members of my local club, the BMW Bikers of Metropolitan Washington, will gather at an assigned location for a surgical session. The patients range from ancient R to modern K bikes, and even an occasional R11 model will show up in the operating room. The surgeons wear beat-up blue jeans and confident smiles.

It is the Slack Pack, the creation of Don Graling. He stole the concept from Gary Smith's Shack Pack in Pittsburgh, who in turn may have stolen the idea from Jan Hofman's Airheads in San Diego. Don altered the name slightly to avoid a copyright-infringement suit, for Smith is not only one of the legends of shade-tree wrenching in Steel City but is also an accomplished shyster.

I was reasonably sure that this project wasn't going to work within a 50-mile radius of the White House, where most of our members seem to be more skillful in shuffling papers and sending faxes than in replacing seals or rejetting carbs. I was even more certain that our three nearby BMW dealers would be greatly irritated that incompetent amateurs would be skirmishing around the sacred battleground held by their authorized mechanics.

In those views I could not have been more wrong. Given the apathy that infects any sort of proposed meeting from a high-school glee club to the National Security Council, the Slack Pack has been a staggering success. Perhaps it is the camaraderie that comes with the fear that if you start dismantling a functioning bike, you might end up walking home;

maybe it is the tiny shiver of delight that arises as you watch a fellow human about to make a catastrophic, expensive mistake; perhaps it is the mere satisfaction of having saved a few bucks.

For such a venture to avoid crashing on takeoff, a few essentials are required. First, a savior must appear and beckon for his disciples to follow. That was Graling. He's good at that. Second, a selfless fool must offer a house and garage to be trashed by the oil-riddled prints, both paw and hoof, of biker scum. That, too, was Graling, whose wife, Lynn, seems positively cheerful at the prospect of her beautiful home being destroyed systematically. Third, a fair assortment of weird tools should be available, such as some 12 mm wrenches and No. 2 flat-bladed screwdrivers. Yes, Graling yet again, who has them all, in addition to things that the Sears catalog has overlooked or never knew about.

But most vital of all would be the presence of someone who actually knew what he was doing, a chief of surgery as it were. Theoretically, I could be such a person, having survived five months at the American Motorcycle Institute and still possessing a Class II BMW certified wrench license. The truth is that since medical school I have confined my practice to a few of the more esoteric specialty areas — spoke cleaning, tire-pressure adjustments — so I really am not the sort of overall expert who is required. The Pack somehow knows this and kindly does not mention it in my presence.

Capital Cycle's Frank Cooper eventually stepped forward. Despite the harried look that perpetually darkens his face, a visage undoubtedly acquired by dealing daily with customers angered that Frank doesn't have the reflux engagement bivalve for a 1925 R32 in stock, he is an island of tranquility in a storm-tossed sea. Without him, or a person of similar capability, even a gentle, laid-back Slack Pack could twist into a Taut Mob in a matter of minutes. Best of all, Frank knows what he doesn't know, and when to step back, priceless talents in any mechanic.

The especially eager neophyte wrenches arrive at seven o'clock on the dot to guarantee decent operating space in Graling's two-car garage. Other bikes begin to pile up in the reception room on the driveway. Tools are laid out, Clymer manuals are opened, and ailing motorcycles are anesthetized. K-bike splines are this season's surgery *du jour.* Soon the swingarm of every other bike in the garage is swinging freely. As driveshafts are slipped from the transmission, anxious surgeons stare at anatomical structures hitherto unknown to them.

"Should this be rusty?" No.

"These splines are squared off. Is that good?" Yes.

"How much grease do I put on these splines?" A thin coating will do. But clean that old crap off there first. I mean *really* clean it.

"Does anyone have any BMW No. 10 grease?" In my pocket.

A fellow has released his bike's fork tubes and now approaches one of the seals with a screwdriver so large that it could pry truth out of Hillary Clinton. I snap to terrified attention.

"How much does that slider cost?" I ask. He doesn't know. "I ask because if you get one inch closer to it with that screwdriver, you're going to be buying one. Let me tell you why." I tell him. The right tool for the right job. Nothing ever was more true. If you don't have it, you're just scrambling. Ultimately that will result in a sack for a 15-yard loss. You lose the game, the cheerleader stops dating you, and your life becomes immeasurably poorer. Because of a stinking screwdriver.

Soon the bikes begin to revive, the hamburger grill shuts down, and the surgeons begin to wash the blood off their shoes. A few people have found problems that are going to require the services of real experts; most have attacked the patient's illness frontally, treated it, and are now sitting back with a smile that says, "Yeah, the patient is going to be fine, but not as fine as I feel right now." Medicare should be so successful.

It strikes me that a motorcycle club can rarely have greater value than this, to afford the opportunity for like-minded people to come together, to learn, to do, and to teach. Humanity's rich history of bloodshed and villainy can almost be forgotten when the Slack Pack or the Shack Pack or a few Airheads convene to get their collective hands filthy. Almost.

The Bubba Brigade

PHOTO CREDIT: MARK HULL

To protect and serve

Like most wretched ideas, this one didn't seem so bad at the time: Let's have the annual BMW Riders Association rally at Fontana Village in Graham County, North Carolina, a state where barnyard pigs outnumber humans six to one, even if you count Jesse Helms two million times. It's close to Deal's Gap, we have a license to sell beer in a dry county, and it's still legal to consummate a marriage to your 10-year-old sister on the courthouse steps. What could go wrong?

Plenty, as Ed Jorgensen, RA's president, began to find out two days before the rally started. Summoned hurriedly to a meeting that had obviously been planned well in advance, he was confronted by representatives of a half-dozen protect-and-serve agencies including North Carolina state, county, and local rent-a-goon squads, the Tennessee Valley Authority, and the Tennessee Highway Patrol, the latter so completely lost that they didn't even know what jurisdiction they were in. The only thugs missing were the elite shock troops from the J. Edgar Hoover Flying Squad of cross-dressing pederasts. Jorgensen hadn't seen such a display of force since he'd been called up as a reservist in the Gulf War. Staring at him from the far end of the conference table were the red, watery eyes of the descendants of the Gadarene swine.

It was short and sweet. The beer license was gone. If you want suds, hike on over to Bryson City, the nearest wet town, just a 70-mile round trip through the deer-infested Smokies. Roadblocks would be established to shake down vehicles with fewer than three wheels. Campers on federal land would have their tents rousted by the slack-jawed, minimum-wage TVA brown shirts who'd be looking for Uzis, switchblades, and heroin, items no true BMW rider ever is without.

Jorgensen could barely ask why.

Easy. They'd received a tip from a reliable informant — stop me if this is beginning to sound suspiciously like the lame excuse that prompted the Spartanburg cop riot two years ago — that some Harley "one-percenters" were headed to Fontana to kick the quiche out of the BMW rallyists. And when the panheads were through, anyone left standing would be finished off by "our own local redneck bikers."

Now normally a BMW rider won't fight about anything, unless the Chablis isn't chilled. But this grotesque explanation makes a kind of rat-like sense, particularly to some ankle-biting cop whose mother couldn't get a role in *Deliverance* because she was too realistic for the part. The lawmen will defuse a gang war by disarming the victims, hassle 2,200 people who propose to spend a million bucks in this backwater sinkhole over the course of four days, threaten the resort owner with a tax audit if he doesn't shut his yap, and do it with such utter disregard of the First and Fourth Amendments that they must believe the Supreme Court is where Duke plays basketball.

"We've been Bubbacized," one rally official groaned. Graham County's sheriff just smiled his vacant smile, thinking this was going to be the biggest thing to hit his patch of Tobacco Road since Lulu Lumley proved that you really can produce a bilious green from blue and yellow crayons.

They might possess less imagination than a sack of cow pies and be three times dumber, but they were at least true to their word. On the first morning of the rally a helicopter strafed the resort with its loudspeaker pounding out "Bad Boys," the theme from the *Cops* TV show. Checkpoints appeared. Dope-sniffing dogs, some bearing a remarkable genetic resemblance to their masters, hustled from one saddlebag to the next. The TVA Gestapo poked at tents. They set up a command center where they sat around day and night in a pathetic boredom that only near-zero IQs can produce, eating doughnuts, whistling

Dixie, and lighting farts.

No Harley gang appeared, of course, apparently having been frightened off by the hopeless stupidity of the entire scene.

Occasionally the stereotype scores a bulls-eye. The roadhouse at the eastern end of the Deal's Gap road advertises itself as "The Crossroads of Time." That's true. It is the intersection of the 11th and 12th centuries, A.D. The richly deserved reputation of the Southern fat-assed, mush-mouthed, pot-bellied, dim-witted, tobacco-drooling, badge-toting caricature of Deputy Dawg was reinforced at Fontana with a vengeance. Their daddies were training fire hoses on demonstrators in Birmingham, their granddaddies were lynching uppity blacks in Selma. They have the indelible mark of the truly and unrepentantly stupid upon their thick, furrowed brows: They simply cannot learn from experience.

That's too bad, because if they had the brains of a smoked catfish they'd see what would happen next. Some civil suits will be filed and eventually won. The county commissioners will issue an apology that might contain some correctly spelled words. BMW of North America will avoid press introductions within a 500-mile radius of western Carolina for the next 50 years. And the county sheriff will soon join the former police chief of Spartanburg, as they wait in the unemployment line, licking chicken grease off their stubby fingers.

One day memories of this bedlam will fade, perhaps by the time Lulu Lumley has worked her way up to watercolors. The ragtag morons masquerading as police officers may one day find some adult supervision. And, because it was a pleasant event despite determined efforts to destroy it, people may want to forget.

I won't.

[Postscript: The Graham County sheriff principally responsible for the fiasco was not, as I predicted, fired for cause. Instead he was indicted the following year for sexual assault and murder threats. He committed suicide before he could be tried.]

Turkey

PHOTO CREDIT: THE AUTHOR

The Cappadocia region of Turkey

As we picked up his bikes in Durusu, a suburb 30 miles northwest of Istanbul, Paolo asked me how fast I'd like to ride back to the city. "Two hundred K," I said. It was a joke, of course. That's 125 mph, roughly twice the speed at which my nose begins to bleed uncontrollably. His question was probably rhetorical anyway. He rolled out of the gas station on his Ninja and I followed on the R11GS. The next time I looked at my speedometer, it was inching toward 180 kph. I decided not to look at it again.

At that speed, in heavy traffic on the outskirts of a city of 10 million people, history is somewhat difficult to absorb. I'd had a glimpse of the city's ruined walls on the way in from the airport a couple of days earlier. Even today they're incredible. Built to repel any attacker, for 1,100 years they had done just that. Then the Ottomans came.

Europe stops at the Bosphorus, a narrow strait 20 miles long and no more than two miles wide, connecting the Black Sea to the north with the Sea of Marmara to the south. You stand on the western shore and imagine you could reach Asia with an easy three-iron.

The area reeks with geopolitical significance. To go east — to Persia, India, and China — you either row across the Bosphorus for a few minutes or walk around the top of the Black Sea for six weeks. If you're a Russian czar, the stakes are even higher. The Bosphorus is your navy's only escape route from the Black Sea to the Aegean, the Mediterranean, and the rest of the Seven Seas.

In 324 A.D. the Roman emperor Constantine took one look at the place, then the ancient Greek city of Byzantium, renamed it after himself, and made it his eastern capital. Walls were erected, three deep with towers 60 feet high, behind an outer moat. With water to the north, east, and south and with four miles of walls to the west, Constantinople laughed at marauding barbarians unskilled at siege warfare. Huns and Visigoths bounced off the massive barrier like BBs. By the end of the first millennium, Constantinople, with a population of one million, the seat of orthodox Christianity and the capital of the Byzantine empire, was the largest city in the known world. We owe it a debt: During the darkest days of the middle ages, the city preserved European culture from extinction.

Nothing lasts forever. Ottoman Turks at the beginning of the 14th century began picking off pieces of the Byzantine realm. Within 150 years all that remained was Constantinople, a head without a body. In the spring of 1453 Sultan Mehmet II rolled up to the walls with 150,000 troops, cut off access to the sea, and ordered the city to surrender or die. Withered by age and corruption and shunned by Europe for its refusal to submit to the pope in Rome, the city — its soldiers outnumbered 20-to-1 — was clearly doomed. Still, Constantinople ignored the Turk, who then began hammering the ancient walls with "Basilica," a 19-ton cannon that shot a projectile weighing 800 pounds, and scores of smaller artillery pieces.

On the 50th day of siege the city fell. Mehmet went directly to the Santa Sophia church and converted it to a mosque. The Byzantine empire, like Rome before it, officially lay in ruins.

But, as I said, at 180 kph the only ruins I was thinking about were my own.

Mike Kneebone and I were in Turkey as the guests of the One More Mile Riders of Istanbul. The invitation, in all candor, had been directed to Mike in his capacity as the president of the Iron Butt Association, but I had earlier advised him to avoid foreign travel without his attorney present to prevent intrigue, plots, and insecure food preparation. I therefore packed, as duty required.

The OMM riders apparently have not yet heard that there is economic chaos — I'd call a persistent inflation rate of two percent per day chaotic, wouldn't you? — in the land formerly known as Anatolia. These guys ride big, new, expensive bikes (invariably BMWs), fill closets with Aerostich clothes, pay $300 a year to wear the club's logo, have studied engineering at MIT, and collect toys even Batman would envy. They speak English better than you do, plus a half-dozen other languages. "Thank you" is *teşekkür ederim*, but you're just as likely to hear *merci*.

They make things, export them, and run the companies that import what they don't want to make. One OMM rider has a 90-percent share of the Turkish battery market. Another, I was told, sets the price of tomatoes on the London commodities exchange every morning. I asked him if it was true. He shook his head and quietly said, "No." Pause. "Paris."

The founder of this remarkable group is Paolo Volpara, an expatriate Italian and retired advertising mogul. He barks out directions to his flock — to you they are captains of Turkish industry but Paolo sees only unruly, fifth-grade boys — stares malevolently if any fails to pay attention, whistles to quiet side conversations, and quotes Mussolini should the need arise: "If I advance, follow me; if I retreat, kill me."

He will never leave his adopted homeland, knee-deep as it is in history, religion, myth, and culture. Turkey was made for a man like Paolo, the namesake of Paul of Tarsus, born here nearly 2,000 years ago. It is too bad that the two Pauls never met; I think it would be great fun to see them debate such weighty matters as whether it actually is better to marry than to burn or whether putting away childish things is such a good idea after all. They are both philosophers, only one is a saint and the other rides the absolute piss out of a motorcycle.

A couple of years ago Paolo came across Mike's Iron Butt Association web site and began thinking of long-distance challenges that might be cooked up in Turkey. He and Mike traded emails for a while. Paolo then set out to grab a Bun Burner Gold award from the IBA, a documented 1,500-mile ride in under 24 hours. No problem.

He followed that with a solo jaunt to the four corners of Turkey, a country 13 percent larger than the state of Texas. He took just four days, a record that will undoubtedly stand for some time, seeing temperatures from sub-freezing to over 100 degrees. Then he began preaching the joys of Iron Butt to any motorcyclist he could find. That eventually led to Mike's being invited in the first week of June of this year to give a talk to the OMM crew about long-distance riding and to over-see an attempt by seven motorcyclists on six bikes for a mass SaddleSore — 1,000 miles in 24 hours — starting and ending in Istanbul.

Mike could not resist such an invitation, of course, nor could his attorney.

> *Every gal in Constantinople*
> *Lives in Istanbul, not Constantinople.*
> *So if you've got a date in Constantinople*
> *She'll be waiting in Istanbul.*

That is from a song popular when I was a kid. It doesn't tell you everything you need to know about one of the world's most fascinating cities, but it's a start. To understand the real schizophrenia of Turkey and its largest city, look at a map.

In the extreme northwest you see a triangle with its apex, Istanbul, pointing east. The city straddles both sides of the Bosphorus. The area of that triangle represents just three per-cent of the entire country's land mass. It is the European part. Everything else to the east and south is Asia. That's the prob-lem: Turkey has never been able to decide whether it wants to be European or Asian, so it tries to be both. Sometimes that works; sometimes it doesn't.

First there were Hittites, then Greeks, Romans, Byzan-tines, Seljuk Turks, and finally Ottoman Turks. By the end of the first world war and the collapse of the Ottoman empire, Constantinople was deemed to be so decadent that Mustafah Kemal Atatürk, the nation's greatest hero and first democratic president, moved the capital to Ankara and renamed the ancient capital Istanbul. That's where your date is waiting.

She'll probably be waiting quite a while, too, because you're almost certainly stuck in traffic, traffic the likes of which you cannot and dare not imagine, traffic that singes the human soul. I have ridden a motorcycle in Mexico City, the most populous place on Earth; it is *nothing* compared to Istanbul. And on Saturday night vehicular motion almost ceases, particularly near the Bosphorus. For over an hour, including 20 miserable minutes sitting on the side of the road waiting for the R11GS to stop overheating, Mike and I struggled to ride five miles from a restaurant to our hotel, splitting lanes, riding on sidewalks, and generally acting like fools the entire time. When I lie on my death bed, my fervent hope will be that it is not in Istanbul on Saturday night, otherwise I may never get off this Earth.

On June 7 we arrived and OMM took us to dinner. The next day OMM rider Orkan Erhan took us on an all-day tour of Topkapi Palace, Aya Sophia, the Blue Mosque, and the awesome Roman cistern that broods under the city. We skipped the grand bazaar because we have all seen outlet malls before. That evening OMM fed us, and Mike blessed the departure of the six SaddleSore bikes, and delivered his Iron Butt lecture to a rapt audience of OMM club members.

On the following day Mike blessed the return of five of the SaddleSore bikes. The sixth rider had been detained by problems of the suspended permit sort. Traffic stops are a way of life in Turkey, as are subsequent license revocations. Many of our compatriots understandably carried multiple licenses from various countries. The cops played their games; the riders played theirs.

Formal duties thus concluded, it was time for a little ride. Paolo warned us to be ready to leave on the morning of

June 11. He used the phrase, "Wheels roll at dawn," and he wasn't smiling. Mike and I looked at each other bleakly and went straight to bed without cookies.

Our travel plan amounted basically to a circumnavigation of the western half of the country, an area approximately the size of the state of California. We had a week to do it.

The motorway putting Istanbul's clotted traffic mercifully behind us was a fine, monotonous highway, as interstate-like roads must by law be. Still, we made good time. Paolo is the soul of concentration on a bike, boring down the road like a diamond bit cutting through steel. Larry Grodsky, *Rider's* safety editor, and Kneebone ride like this too. I grow tired and pissed off watching such people never make mistakes.

Just beyond Tekirdağ, a cop waved us over. Paolo was boiling before his bike even came to rest. We'd been dinged for speeding, I guessed, but it wasn't that. We'd allegedly ignored a double yellow line on a highway so long, straight, and empty that you could almost see Greece at the end of it. *Oh, please,* I thought. *Not this early in the game.* Paolo somehow convinced the cop that his important American guests were not about to stand for this unspeakable crap, so just back the hell off. And the cop backed the hell off.

Late in the morning I saw a sign: Gelibolu 10 km. You know this place as Gallipoli, a town at the northern end of a narrow peninsula, from the movie of the same name starring a young Mel Gibson. Historians recall it as the place where Winston Churchill, the first lord of the British Admiralty during the Great War, had a really bad time of it. He had hoped to run gunboats up the Dardanelles — through which practically every drop of rain that falls on western Asia eventually exits into the Mediterranean — seize Constantinople (as Istanbul was then known), and knock Turkey out of the war. Good plan; bad execution. The Turks held the high ground all over the peninsula and easily repelled every Allied attempt to come off the beaches. I love crime scenes. This was one I couldn't miss.

Ephesus, one of the Seven Wonders of the ancient world

The Anzac Cove, where Australian and New Zealand soldiers were bottled up and shredded for endless weeks, was an
even sadder and gloomier place than I had feared. You stand
on the beach and look up to the cliffs where the entrenched

enemy waits. You've come halfway around the world and it is suddenly obvious that you will never get out of this terrible place alive. It was a bad time to be young and speak English.

A few miles south of Çannakale lie the ruins of Troy and the ghosts of people so familiar to us that even 23 centuries later they don't need last names: Alexander, Aristotle, Helen, and Homer, who, for all we know about the poet, might have been a man, two men, a woman, or a boy with a chicken and a bloodthirsty sense of style.

A replica — I'm sure it isn't the real thing — of the giant wooden horse that the treacherous Greeks brought here stands at the entrance to the shattered town. It is impressive. If a Greek showed up at my gates with such a creature, I'd let him in too.

Mike and I wandered around for a while. There are ruins and there are ruins, and the ruins at Troy are truly ruined. I couldn't bond with the place at all. Paolo, having been through the site too often already, stayed with the bikes and thought the thoughts that people like Paolo think. When we came out, he was writing meticulous entries into a diary with the same tiny script that Eugene O'Neill favored before going completely insane.

"Helen's beauty was great enough to launch a thousand ships," I said casually. Paolo narrowed his eyes. I asked if he knew what a milli-Helen was. He narrowed his eyes further still. "It's the beauty required to launch one ship," I said. He tried not to laugh.

In Assos we sat in a hotel restaurant and looked out to the sea at twilight. Three thousand years ago Phoenician sailors had come ashore here to wench the night away. St. Paul might have had a beer at the bar, before he became a saint, naturally. On top of a hill above us were the remains of a Roman city. I complained that the intensity of the country's history was giving me a headache. Ignoring my pain, Paolo asked if I could name the Seven Wonders of the World.

"Of course," I said wearily. "The Great Pyramid of Giza. The Colossus of Rhodes. The Hanging Gardens of Babylon. The Lighthouse at Alexandria. The Temple of Zeus at Olympia. The Yankee Stadium of the Bronx. And Domino's thin-crust pepperoni pizza."

"The Temple of Artemis at Ephesus and the Mausoleum at Halicarnassus. Do you realize that we could be at those places, as well as Rhodes, by noon tomorrow?"

My head throbbed. I couldn't remember the Turkish word for "aspirin."

It's as simple as this: If you travel on Turkish roads, you're going to have close encounters of the cop kind. A rider in Istanbul's One More Mile club told me that in a single day's trip from the north coast to the Mediterranean, he netted four separate speeding tickets without ever really burning up the pavement. Routes plodded by tourists are disproportionately selected for enforcement, since tourists generally have a lot more money than the locals but lack the language skills to bitch effectively. Our second encounter with the police in as many days, this one a radar trap on the outskirts of Edremit, left us each 27 million lira poorer. It sounds bad, but it amounted essentially to just a tank of gas for the GS. Fortunately, it's a pay-as-you-go routine, so we paid and went. Nothing personal.

As Istanbul was once Constantinople, and Bodrum once Halicarnassus, so Izmir was once Smyrna, with a history dating to the Bronze Age. For the motorcyclist, it is, like all industrial open sores, a place to avoid at all costs. We did our best and continued south to Ephesus, the prime tourist magnet in the country. Over the centuries the sea has retreated westward from the ruins, forcing Mediterranean love boats now to tie up at the port of Kuşadasi. Tour buses without number roll in during the summer months, turning the parking lot into a miniature Izmir, a place you smell before you see.

Despite the crowds and the noise, if Ephesus doesn't step

you back, nothing in Turkey will. Paolo put on his guide hat and began dragging me around. He explained history, architecture, farming methods, religious practices, culture, butterfly ballots, and Planck's constant. Even I could appreciate what this place must have been like in its heyday. It had been the center of St. Paul's missionary activity for three years. Aristotle taught here. The library lacks only scrolls. The ruts of Roman chariot wheels are visible in the marble streets. My head swam.

And here once stood a massive temple dedicated to the goddess of the hunt, Diana for the Romans or Artemis for the Greeks, depending upon which civilization was on top. It was one of the Seven Wonders of the World. Today, like the crumbling statute in Shelley's poem *Ozymandias*, "nothing beside remains." Indeed, of those ancient wonders only the pyramids still stand. Given enough time and the laws of thermodynamics, everything is destined to vanish, I suppose, except re-runs of *I Love Lucy*.

I remember little of the remainder of the ride that day except that we were in mountains for about eight years and that it was ridiculously hot for such a spring afternoon. We eventually climbed into the hills above the coastal village of Goçek where Paolo and his wife share a summer retreat with angry, black scorpions large enough to pay rent. We stayed in Goçek for two nights, visiting ruins in the hills above Fethiye and wandering along back roads near the mountainous coast. It was the most beautiful part of Turkey that we would see. We stopped for lunch in a village. Across the road on a hillside were hundreds of ageless stone hovels. Roman soldiers might have slept there.

"Do you know where most of those people wound up?" Paolo asked.

"Izmir," I said, my idea of hell.

"Chicago," Mike said, his idea of heaven.

"Mike's right," Paolo said. It had been a working-class Greek village. For some reason in the 1920s everyone packed up, headed west, and became Cubs fans. It was a microcosm of the history of the Mediterranean and Aegean coastlines. Phoenicians, Lycians, Greeks, Romans, Venetians, and now Turks, one after the other. When I was a kid, Cyprus was on fire; tomorrow the flames will be someplace else. Half the coastal towns have two or more names. You really can't tell the players without a scorecard. When in doubt, and I was *always* in doubt, I looked for an arch, which meant that a Roman engineer had been there. The old Greeks calculated the circumference of the Earth with astonishing accuracy, but the simple keystone arch eluded them to the very end.

We left Goçek for a day's ride north to Ankara, the capital, to meet some riders from a local bike club for dinner. Paolo has been recruiting them to The Way of Iron Butt. They toasted Paolo. Paolo toasted them back. Mike was toasted royally as a visiting fireman and happily returned the favor. Soon everybody was toasting the absolute hell out of everybody else. Still, in the cab on the way back to our hotel after dinner, the drunkest guy in the car was the taxi driver.

Wheels rolled early to the unearthly region of Cappadocia, a bizarre geology of lava and sandstone, the purest kind of badlands. Into such inhospitable climes came early Christians to live in caves, paint ethereal Biblical scenes on the walls and ceilings, and formulate basic religious doctrines that survive to this day. One group of early settlers, escaping enemies, burrowed like moles to form an eight-story city beneath the earth.

Late in the afternoon, just before closing time, we tried to enter an enormous church-cave. The ticket agent, a government stooge, turned us away. Too late, he said. Clearly we were not. The battle thus was joined. You have not lived until you've seen apoplectic Turks swearing purple oaths and screaming death threats at each other about whether a primitive Christian church should be open or not. Half an hour later a dozen of us came to a restaurant that was just closing for the night.

Is it too late for dinner, we asked? The owner took one look at $150,000 worth of motorcycles in his lot and, with a big smile, tossed the "Closed" sign on the floor.

Murad Acar toasted Mike and me at our last dinner in an ancient Greek restaurant. Honor to have us. Wonderful to meet such nice guys. Hope you return. I can't remember half the nice things he said. Then it was my turn for a toast.

"When I told my long-suffering Susan that Mike and I were coming to Turkey, she tried not to laugh. She had visited here five years ago and returned to the U.S. a changed person. Clearly she had no such hopes for Mike and me. 'You will not learn even two words of Turkish,' she predicted.

"Mike and I have ridden around much of the world, but we are here to tell you tonight that we have never been with such kind, generous, considerate hosts as we have found in the One More Mile riders. We have never been surrounded by such history. You are lucky. You live in a magnificent country in an amazing part of the world. We will never be able to thank you enough for sharing it with us as you have done.

"And when I go home, I will tell Susan of the things that we saw and did and heard here. I will also tell her that she was wrong. I did learn two words of Turkish: *Teşekkür ederim.* Thank you."

ON THE LEVEL – AUGUST 2006

Perfect

(L-R) Ted Simon and Robert Hellman

For some years now I have taken it upon myself to procure the principal speakers at the Square Route Rally, the annual bash of the BMW Bikers of Metropolitan Washington. I could invite mechanics or bike dealers or judges or racers or designers or motor cops or safety instructors or bureaucrats who hold our future in their sweaty hands. I never do. I look for writers. As a result, we've had Ted Simon, Patrick Symmes, Simon Milward, and Greg Frazier as guests. One year in a moment of desperation I invited myself.

While it is almost holy writ, so to speak, that you should never meet a writer whom you admire, this year I called upon Melissa Pierson, the author of *The Perfect Vehicle*. To understand why she was at the top of my list of motoscribes you need read nothing more than this, two sentences from one of the introductory chapters:

> From my mother I learned to write prompt
> thank-you notes for a variety of occasions; from
> Mrs. King's ballroom dancing school I learned
> a proper curtsey and, believe it or not, what to
> do if presented with nine eating utensils at the
> same place setting, presumably at the home of
> the hosts to whom I had just curtsied. From
> motorcycles I learned practically everything else.

Trust me here: Writing doesn't get any better than that. I could teach a college course in expository writing using nothing but that paragraph. It is a jewel, a brilliantly polished gem, that lights up the table for the nine-course dinner that follows.

And what a dinner it is. The author leads us through the history of motorcycles, their construction, their allure, and their peril. Someone someday somehow may write as good a book about *what it is about motorcycles* — the perfect subtitle of Pierson's book — but none will write the story better.

At the outset, something about the machine appeals to a primitive part of her soul. She can't resist it. This is a literary psychodrama on so many different levels of understanding that it would be incomprehensible except for this simple fact: You and I have been there too. We looked at the bike. We had to have it. So we know what she's saying. We relate. Even people who haven't heard that siren call screaming in their ears can appreciate what is happening.

She buys a Guzzi, learns to ride it, to work on it, to meet friends on it, and to make it a part of her life. Her reflections are those of a post-novice motorcyclist channeling experiences through a master storyteller and craftsman. She tosses wonderful facts at us (*e.g.*, seven million ride bikes but three times that many watch birds) and repeatedly pops us with a brilliant turn of phrase ("Let's call him Tad, and me ready.").

Additionally, she may have been the luckiest writer who ever lived, coming at her subject while still innocent enough to appreciate the machine's uncommon attraction, but not yet battered by its hellish risks. She thus managed to capture lightning in a bottle in this amazing, beautiful work. If it is the only book about bikes you ever read, it will be enough.

Given the scarcity of motorcycle-oriented titles published each year, and the even more rare genius of composition in that genre, I expected that the book's appearance almost 10 years ago would have generated universal acclaim. It came close, but there was something about Pierson's acknowledgment of the approach-avoidance problem inherent in the bike's very essence that caused a ripple of discontent among biker-poets who are forever scribbling doggerel about their trusty steeds.

Melissa wasn't having any of that. She knew the steed wasn't worthy of a shred of trust, something that is intuitively obvious to anyone who has ever ridden a one-track vehicle. This thing, she wrote bluntly, can kill you faster than the emergency response team can peel you off the grill of a Volvo. Sure, it's a machine of exceptional beauty, function, and lineage, but you're never going to escape its physics. In the end it is going to do whatever it takes to wind up on its side.

Still, she said, if you can learn to handle this thing, to tame it like an unruly horse, surviving the elemental danger of the enterprise may be enough to offset the downside risks. Staring death in the face and coming out smiling has always been, and will always be, the straight flush in life's poker game.

This yin and yang is the dark midnight of motorcycling's soul. No one in the trade writes about it. It is the distant bell that is heard only by the unconscious mind. And no motorcyclist wants to hear it anyway. You don't go into the garage each morning and ask that shiny machine, "Is this the day you kill me, you bitch?" You already know the answer: It will if it can. You're supposed to be the master, so master it, if you can.

They tell us we can. Read the safety books, go to the safety classes, wear the safety equipment. Think safety, ride safely, be safe. And then the news comes through the motorcycle community like an electric current: Larry Grodsky, Mr. Safety himself, has been killed by a deer. He was as good as they come; he could manage any risk; and we buried him nonetheless. If he can't make it, what chance do the rest of us have? Only the security of a dice roll.

This, I think, is the ultimate complaint with the subtext of Pierson's book. If you know how bad it is and you do it anyway, aren't you just asking for it? Isn't this the very definition of a death wish? And if all you want to do is die, just do it and shut the hell up. Why write a book about it?

There is a kind of sophomoric, *post hoc* logic to the argument, I admit, but Pierson's few critics are missing the larger point. She's telling the truth. There really is a clear and present danger in the game. You accept it? Fine. So do I. We know the score. And if it were only us, we could just put on the blinders, go back to the steed poetry, and take our chances. But there are others knocking at the door.

Thirty years ago my brother and I took a three-week road trip in a VW Beetle around the country. It has become, as *On the Road* adventures often do, the stuff of family legend. The other day my brother's son, now 18, asked me if the three of us were going to repeat the trip next summer, but this time on motorcycles.

"You don't have a bike endorsement," I dodged, hearing a distant bell.

"I can get one before the sun goes down," he said.

He could, I know. And I could send him through the MSF beginner and experienced courses, shove bike rags down his throat, and dress him in Andy Goldfine's finest armored Cordura nylon. I can teach him all he knows, but I can never teach him all I know. That gap could one day be a fatal abyss. Thus comes my yin-yang moment: I accept living on the edge like a Flying Wallenda, but I recoil from putting someone who trusts me on the tightrope.

I don't know how this will turn out. Living in a bunker makes me pessimistic. Maybe the kid won't even like a motorcycle. That would solve everything. In the meantime, I've been thinking about a Christmas present for him. I know a good book. It would be the perfect gift.

MOTORCYCLE CONSUMER NEWS – JANUARY 1995

Clarence Thomas and Me
Or, Here Commences the Education of
Absolutely the World's Worst Motorcycle Mechanic

The author as a BMW Class II certified mechanic-in-training

Day 1
11.11.94

I intend to learn to be a wrench, though it is far from clear to me that an old dog can learn new tricks. I've never had an old dog; they all died before learning much of anything. I do know that you can't teach a cat any worthwhile tricks, no matter how old it is. For 14 years I've been trying to teach my cat, Bud, to say "chainsaw." But she's never said a word, at least not while I was around.

The learning process theoretically is straightforward: You learn from your parents. My mother taught me that an orange necktie doesn't go with anything; my father taught me that if you want something done well, pay someone else to do it. Though admittedly this wasn't much with which to start a life, somewhere I discovered that people should always do as adults what they did well as kids. From my earliest days I was a gifted liar and thief, so it was taken for granted that I would eventually go to law school. And I did. For nearly 19 years I practiced law, occasionally getting it right, and sat at a clean desk on spring afternoons watching the blood drain out of my shoes. My life was leaking away, one corpuscle at a time. On Sunday nights, just as the TV movie about yet another victimized woman would begin, I'd notice my stomach cramping up.

It took me a year to realize it wasn't the movie that was

The author rides away from work for the last time.

turning my gut into a peptic Chernobyl; it was the prospect of going to the courthouse the next day, trying a case that Clarence Darrow couldn't win, and listening to more lawyer jokes, all of which were true.

It was enough. I told my partner that if I'd been convicted of first-degree murder I wouldn't have had to serve 19 years. Thus, at the age of 52.8, I retired, leaving the law in the grubby hands of sanctimonious ankle-biters like Joel Hyatt. To hell with him, I thought. I had a better plan. I would ride a motorcycle around the world. Not many people have done that. Those who did — and I have talked with some of them — usually had either lots of time or money. I had both. I could do it.

One little problem remained: After 352,000 miles and 33 years in the saddle, I still didn't know how to change a flat tire. When I take a trip, the owner's manual is always nearby; I worry that I may forget how to put gas in the tank. On really big trips I always try to carry Mike Kneebone with me; he's plugged my tires in barren deserts from Nevada to Australia. But asking him to drop his family, friends, and career for a couple of years to wrench me around the world could be a bit of an imposition.

Incompetence at my level doesn't come cheaply. It takes a lifetime of real work to accumulate enough money to pay other people to do everything all the time, generally at time-and-a-half, because among my other faults I'm also impatient. But I did it. I'd taken my father's advice and I'd learned to pay. And now, when the survivors of World War III begin crawling out of their holes to rebuild their lives, I'll just remain in my fall-out shelter and die quietly. With the banks and my Visa card reduced to radioactive dust, I'd be more belly-up than fish on 42nd Street. Rebuild a carburetor? Hell, I can't rebuild a good burp.

Unfortunately, with a proposed world jaunt, I have come up against a wall that I cannot buy my way over. When the bike crumps in Wadi Al-Zahir, 14 kilometers from the epicenter of the Gobi Desert, there may be nobody around to pay. What then, Bobby baby? Calamity has struck better men and women than I. Ted Simon changed a piston in the Sahara; Steve Attwood, the '93 Iron Butt winner, fixed 10 flats in one month alone in India; Tabitha Estabrook, during a monster ride with her fiancé, Wall Street financier Jim Rogers, hand cut a set of cylinder studs borrowed from a Russian tractor in central Siberia. Rogers, who freely confesses that his mechanical ability is no better than mine, stood on the far side of the road, looking in vain for someone to take his money.

Two years ago I discovered a possible way out. In an article in *Motorcycle Consumer News*, Vince Iorio described a school, the American Motorcycle Institute in Daytona Beach, that claimed it could take almost anyone and in 20 weeks transform the subject into an entry-level mechanic. The operative word there is "almost." AMI hadn't met me, and I wasn't sure it would want to.

Although I am morbidly shy, when desperation strikes I can occasionally force myself to move off of bottom dead center. Thus, last March, during the Total Raging Hell of Bike Week, I rolled up to the front door of AMI and asked to speak to an admissions officer. Before I could panic and flee, Larry McCarthy showed up and introduced himself.

After a brief tour of the site, we sat down. I admitted that I couldn't stick hose clamps end-to-end; I'd tried once, I said, and I had witnesses who are still laughing about it. Once on a group ride with six friends, when I took a screwdriver out of my tool kit to tighten a bolt or whatever, four of them grabbed their cameras and took pictures. No one had ever seen me use a tool without stabbing myself in the face.

"Not to worry," McCarthy said. "You don't have any bad habits to unlearn."

"I don't have any habits at all," I moaned. "I'd pay *anything* for a good habit."

Some weeks later, I sent in the application. If there was a question about hose clamps, I didn't see it. If I did see it, I didn't answer it. If I did answer it, I lied. Having crested the tender age of 55, it is increasingly difficult for me to deny that middle age is right around the corner. But other leopards with significant lifetime accomplishments have changed their spots — Albert Schweitzer abandoned a career as a university scholar and world-class organist to enter medical school in his thirties; Michael Jordan is now trying to slam dunk outside curve balls; Jeffrey Daumer has modified his diet. I'm a little older, but the principle is still valid, I hope.

And it's not like there's much riding on this, either. Not like the PGA golfer some years ago who supplemented his income by robbing banks. "You think you know what pressure is?" he said as they led him away in handcuffs. "When Nicklaus lines up a putt, he knows that if he misses it, it'll cost him $50,000. I'm thinking that if I miss this damned putt, I'll have to go out and rob another bank."

So in a few weeks when my learning curve begins to describe a flat line (or worse), and the AMI instructors are drawing a chalk outline around my body, who'll know, aside from maybe 75,000 people? It could be worse; I could be Clarence Thomas.

The day is warm. A storm rises miles out at sea. I am sitting on my bike near the front door of AMI, thinking about the last time I appeared to argue a case in the U.S. Court

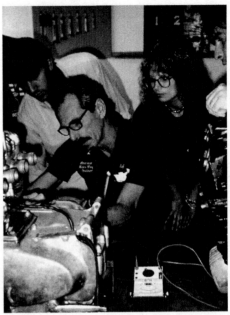

PHOTO CREDIT: THE AUTHOR

AMI instructor Dave Banes with students

of Appeals for the District of Columbia circuit, a farm team for judges on their way to the Supreme Court. Warren Burger came from that bench; so did Antonin Scalia and Robert Bork.

Sitting on the panel are Harry Edwards, Ruth Bader Ginsberg, and Clarence Thomas. Destiny is awaiting Ginsberg and Thomas, though they don't know it. She will skate right up the Big Court, being a Gyno-American with no dirty laundry, but Thomas will spend days defending his taste in porn movies to a captivated audience the length and width of the globe.

I glance at my watch. The first class of the first day starts in five minutes. The butterflies in my gut begin to flap about. It's always the same. The heavyweight lawyers say that you should start worrying when the butterflies go away. Just get the first words out without mangling anything: "May it please the court . . . "

Change places with Clarence? Live that life? Feel the shoes

(L-R) Jim Brown and Norman Hammond

filling up with blood again? Sunday night cramps?

I don't think so.

I walk toward the front door of the school.

Day 59
2.8.95

Every time I start getting depressed about things — today is one of those days — I try to remind myself that I am one of the very few people in the entire school who is never going to earn a dime twisting a wrench for my daily bread. I also try to keep in mind that I've had quite a fortunate life. The world doesn't owe me anything.

For me, my presence at AMI is pretty much a lark. For most of the others, it's the fulfillment of a dream. For a small few this is the last stop if they don't make it. I used to think there was some pressure on me. I've learned better. Pressure? I wouldn't know pressure here if it squeezed my head flat.

Yesterday, another day when I wasn't feeling all that chipper, I was talking to David Harrison at the afternoon break. He's in the Harley program here. Back in the real world he's the co-owner of a dealership in Canada an hour west of Toronto. He's been a pretty fair mechanic for several years but felt that if he could come to school here, he'd be even better. I admire that kind of sacrifice today for goal tomorrow, not the giggling, summer-camp mentality that I brought here. He knows what he's doing and he's serious about it.

David is like most of the students in Class #231. They have

gotten happier with the onset of the hands-on part of the program, disassembling their own or other real motorcycles and reveling in the grease. I'm trying to catch on. But I feel as if I fall further behind each day.

I saw my instructor, Van, heading across the quadrangle. End of break time. Ach. Soon he'll discover that I don't have a clue how to adjust valves on a K bike, despite having been doing it for more than a day.

"Don't get discouraged," David said.

"Not me," I lied.

I headed toward the BMW room; David turned to the Harley lab with a smile. His happiness is evident. He really enjoys those thumping bikes.

I walked a few steps, then turned to watch him. It has always been interesting for me to see how he goes into a room. Grab the door handle, slide back a foot while swinging it open, then dart forward before it can whack him.

He makes it look easy, going through a door in a wheelchair.

Day 100
4.7.95

One hundred times in the last five months I have come home from school, turned on the computer, typed a header line, and told my diary what I learned in school today. A story needs closure. Tonight is that, the final entry.

At 8:00 a.m. the graduates-to-be gathered in a large classroom. When James Watts walked in, someone in the back of the room cranked up Elgar's *Pomp and Circumstance March No. 5* on a boom box. Watts passed out the critique forms. When we'd finished them, we were free to go over to the site of the graduation ceremony. I handed in an 18-page evaluation I'd already prepared and told Watts I'd see him at 11:45, the appointed time, at the beachside Days Inn. I hadn't even

BMW instructor and Iron Butt Rally finisher Van Singley

begun to think about packing.

A lot of this is becoming dim. I remember walking around to the various classrooms and offices, saying goodbye to the teachers and staff who wouldn't be at the ceremony. With the help of a couple of fellow students, I shoved the R80G/S into the back of a U-Haul truck and lashed it to one side. Then I retrieved the Paris-Dakar from the U-Haul parking lot, rode it up the ramp, and tied it down. Finally I returned to the motel, threw everything I owned into some plastic bags, and heaved them into the truck. I made it to the Days Inn only 10 minutes late.

I tried on a couple of occasions to summarize my feelings about this day, but I wasn't having much success. There were too many conflicting and overlaying emotions, too many things left undone, too much to learn in too little time. Though I was eager to get back home, having spent just eight nights in my own bed during the past five months, paradoxically I wasn't eager to leave Daytona.

The last time I felt anything similar to this was five years ago when Mike Kneebone and I emerged from an endless ride through the Australian outback. We had hammered at that unforgivable loneliness with such fervor that we didn't even realize it had subtly taken us prisoners for keeps.

AMI did that to me, and though it took a little longer, it did its work just as efficiently.

Watts handed out the diplomas. Chuck Fort, steady to the end, was the overall winner with 3.60, beating out Jim Brown

(3.54), Joe Snyder (3.52), and me (3.49). With a giant smile José Luna, the Brazilian whose struggles had been the stuff of legend, took his diploma and broadly wiped his brow. Many parents at the banquet looked on proudly as their sons and daughters walked to the front of the room, accompanied by cheering and clapping. My name was the last called. When Watts handed my diploma to me, I dropped to one knee in gratitude; I felt as if I'd been knighted.

"We will make you an entry-level mechanic," Watts had said on that first day so many months earlier. I'd had doubts. But the school did more than that with guys like Jim, Chuck, and Joe. Even the guys who'd run so long on the ragged edge knew infinitely more today about the trade than when they'd arrived. Indeed, I'd been the perfect test case. From someone who didn't know a dial caliper from a micrometer, AMI turned me into a BMW mechanic who just three days ago was offered a job at a dealership. Thus do worms turn.

"Some of the people you will meet here will be your friends for life," Watts had said on that blustery November day. Maybe, I thought. But when I was taking some photos of friends I'd experienced so much with for so long, I knew I'd be seeing them again.

People began filing out of the room. I hung back, savoring the moment. These students had survived a war; many we'd begun with had not. It had been a classical epic, a story line that runs without interruption from Homer's *Odyssey* to Twain's *Huckleberry Finn* to Kerouac's *On the Road*: A youth leaves home, journeys uncertainly through alien, forbidding lands, and returns, hammered in a crucible but wiser.

I made a final stop back at school to say goodbye to the one person I had not seen all day, the school's president and the man who had made my journey possible. Lamar Williams wasn't in his office; he was at the receptionist's desk, filling in. I shook my head and smiled. It was so typical.

"This is not easy for me," I said. "All I can say is that I have never in my life felt such a sense of accomplishment as

Jim Brown, the author's guardian angel at AMI

I do today. I owe you and the staff far more than I can ever tell you."

"You worked hard," he said. "We're proud of you."

"I learned from the best." We shook hands a final time.

A U-Haul truck takes me home, I thought, as I turn onto I-95 northbound. *I could have come home on my shield*. Strange winds blow this way and that.

You never know.

[Postscript: The complete record of my sojourn at AMI can be found on the Iron Butt Association's website: www.ironbutt.org/higdon/higami.htm.]

Ebb and Flow

PHOTO CREDIT: JUDI HUNT

It started with Ted Verrill in July. He was northbound on I-95 to the MOA rally in New York. At the Delaware Memorial Bridge he moved the bike over to the right lane and stared out at the industrial maze to the south on both sides of the stinking, polluted river. He likes this view for some reason. It was very nearly the last thing he ever saw.

Shakespeare said that there is a tide in the affairs of men which, taken at the flood, leads on to fortune. Maybe, but if you catch that wave wrong, it can kill you. The north-shore Hawaiian surf scenes in Bruce Brown's movie *The Endless Summer* would make even the pros from Dover step back. You listen to that D-minor background chord digging into the base of your skull, see those tiny men on tiny boards atop 50-foot waves, and know that the surfer life isn't always what it's cracked up to be.

And there's Verrill, hanging 10 and sucking in the sulfur dioxides from the DuPont factory complex, a boy and his board on a summer morning. Just beyond the crest of the bridge he glances forward and sees that his world is about to come apart. He's closing on stopped traffic at better than 60 mph. In 2/5ths of a second, unless his luck changes dramatically, he is going head first into the back of a flat-bed trailer.

This day he's not lucky. He splatters into that rig, ripping the handlebars off the bike's triple clamp with his hands. That's not easy to do, and he pulverizes both wrists in the effort. Then, before his smashed body has even stopped sliding on the pavement, a following truck runs over him.

It's easier to list the anatomy that wasn't broken, bruised, dented, or crushed than to recite that which was. The paramedics who reached him didn't think he'd make it to the hospital alive. He was taking rapid, tiny breaths, the kind of breathing you do just before you stop breathing altogether.

When he was evacuated to Virginia some weeks later, I visited him in the hospital. I asked him if in that last moment he had reached an understanding of the unified field theory or the meaning of *Finnegan's Wake*. No, he said, and neither did his life pass before his glazed eyes. When the bike ground to an instantaneous stop and launched its owner into a wall of steel, Ted simply said to himself, *"So this is how it ends."* It didn't, but no one really knows why not.

Some weeks later David Morris and Fran Crane died on the same day. A week after that David's wife, grief-stricken, was dead. Robert Hellman told me, "I'm becoming afraid to open mail or answer the phone." Another car wreck killed a high-school classmate of mine as she vacationed in Hungary. That was the toll for just September.

There is a theoretical limit to a wave's height. I think it's about 150 feet. However large it may be, surely it can't go on forever. Sooner or later it must wear itself out or hit something even bigger than it is. On my birthday in late October I was told that another friend from long ago had succumbed to cancer. It was a grim birthday anyway, one evenly divisible by 10. That news just made it worse.

Later the long-suffering Susan tried to console me. "I'll take you to the Pines for dinner," she said. It's our favorite Italian restaurant, with Pakistani owners, Iranian busboys, and Guatemalan cooks. We invited Irv Warden to join us. When he was an hour late, I knew he'd crumped. I felt like Typhoid Mary.

We picked him up the next afternoon at Arlington Hospital and took him home with us. He'd been running his K75 just after dusk. Traffic slammed to a halt. He grabbed for the brake lever but inexplicably missed it. Bang.

Both of his wrists were broken, though not as badly as Ted's had been. It was a small consolation. One wrist in a sling is irritating; two of them *hors de combat* reduce you to a kind of life you cannot recognize. At least Irv could walk. Ted still can't, but God knows he's working at it. His optimism drains me.

In Spanish an ocean wave is *la ola*. I remember the word because it looks and sounds a little like *olé*, the bullfight cheer. I think of a stadium. I see people, 10 years past fashion, still trying to do the wave. I see the bull, bloody and beaten, dazedly wondering how he has come to die in this hot sand. He looks like some of my friends.

Soon it will be December. The Atlantic hurricane season is behind us. The hateful winter storms are coming, but I can survive them, I guess. It's those waves I worry about. I wish they'd stop.

When the Sun Rose Twice

The Trinity site near Alamogordo, New Mexico, in July 1945

I made this reservation in person *seven months ago*," I said to the desk clerk kid at the Crossroads Motel in Carrizozo, New Mexico. "With your mother. Call her. Now."

Mom remembered me. She should have. The Crossroads doesn't get a lot of walk-in motorcycle trade from Washington, D.C. We worked things out, which was just as well, because Billy the Kid used to ride through Carrizozo and I was feeling a bit on the ornery side myself. I needed that motel room. They don't open up the Trinity site every day.

Most of my trips start being planned after three days on the road. Not this one. Last winter, when I heard that on only two days a year visitors are allowed into the zone where the first atomic bomb was exploded, I resolved to be there. I flew into Denver on the last day of September, picked up my BMW K75, the West Coast bike, and headed south.

Those who believe that nothing worth a damn was ever achieved by a committee ought to study the Manhattan Project. That group built The Bomb. It was a work of supreme art, science, and magic. So shrouded in secrecy was the laboratory in Los Alamos, high in the mountains northwest of Santa Fe, that during the war it officially did not even exist.

Robert Oppenheimer, the project's director, needed a quiet, out-of-the-way place to pop the cork on his plutonium baby, the mightiest weapon ever detonated. The army's bombing and gunnery range northwest of Alamogordo was perfect: isolated, yet not too distant from Los Alamos. Today the area is the site of the White Sands Missile Range, bounded roughly by Carrizozo and Socorro to the north, Alamogordo and Las Cruces to the south. It is a tract of undiluted, depopulated desert in an area so unforgiving to travelers that the Spanish conquistadors remembered their trek through the region as Jornada del Muerto, the death march.

Just as slivers of a gray dawn appeared over the Oscura peaks in mid-July, 1945, the sky exploded with a new light. A book reviewer in the *New York Times* later wrote, "Nothing in recorded history — and in legend since Prometheus brought down fire from Olympus — had such a shattering effect on the collective psyche of mankind as did the sudden appearance of the atomic bomb."

It sure had an effect on *my* psyche. I am a member of the "duck and cover" generation, we who were in grade school in the early 1950s, just after Stalin's Commie scientists had learned how to brew a bomb of their own. It was an ugly, psychotic era. Among my collection of yellowed junior-high grade reports and class pictures is a small card with instructions on hunkering under a desk and covering my poor butt against the impending blast. Sure, today's kids are troubled by school bullies who carry 9mm Glocks; but I spent my formative years worrying about *uranium shrapnel* ripping through the window of my social studies class.

By 1953 much of the area around Ground Zero had stopped glowing. A small pilgrimage was permitted into the sector to pray for peace. In ensuing years a tradition grew. Now the place where the rotational axis of the Earth shifted a bit nearly 50 years ago is open to the public on the first Saturdays of April and October.

In mid-morning I rode east on U.S. 380, slowly and lazily, toward Stallion Gate, the north access to the missile range. The desert swam dizzily before me in every direction. It's an hour's ride, and a barren one, from Carrizozo. Even on a busy day there's nothing there.

I pulled up at the gate. The guard handed me a brochure

and a map of the area. "Head south," he said. "When you see an intersection, turn left. Photography is prohibited until you get to the site."

The region has an eerie, sinister aura. I felt like a spy, so as soon as I was out of sight of the guard's kiosk, I stopped and took an illegal picture of the hot, blank landscape. The road was a needle for 15 miles. In the midst of nowhere I saw a military policeman standing in the road. I turned left. A few minutes later I pulled into the parking lot.

Upwards of 500 people were already in the area, walking the short path to and from Ground Zero, buying junk from concessionaires, and possibly considering the proposition that humanity is a branch on the evolutionary tree that has come very close to chopping off its own limb.

Perspiration dripped into my eyes. Trying to survive a July day in this feverish plain was unimaginable. I walked slowly up the dirt path to the perimeter fence, my boots kicking up small clouds of reddish-brown dust. *Giants strode here*, I thought. *Oppenheimer, Fermi, Teller, Feynman, Gamow. You couldn't throw a rock back then without hitting someone who would win a Nobel prize.*

I walked to the lava obelisk which marks The Spot. A four-legged, 100-foot steel tower had stood here, holding the bomb like a delicate child. A twisted fragment of one of the footings was visible in the sand. I wandered over to a display of historical photos and poked around the casing of a replica of Fat Man, the Nagasaki bomb. A low-slung shelter with warped plastic viewports enclosed a small part of the original crater floor. I looked through the panes and saw nothing but old dirt.

Fifteen seconds before 5:30 a.m., Mountain War Time, on July 16, 1945, a light appeared in the desert, a fire brighter than anything ever seen on the planet, so brilliant that it could have been seen with the naked eye from the moon. In a millionth of a second the steel tower turned into gas. The heat produced in an instant was four times greater than at the surface of the sun. Sand melted and bacteria vaporized.

Six miles from the blast, Oppenheimer stood in the control

bunker, thinking of a Hindu poem, the Bhagavad-Gita: *I am become Death, the destroyer of worlds.* There was a small but theoretical chance that the explosion would ignite the atmosphere, incinerating the Earth. He waited and watched.

Eleven hundred miles away, in McComb, Mississippi, I turned in my sleep, unaware at five years that the age of innocence had passed.

I didn't stay long. It's not the world expo; there isn't much to see.

I rode slowly on the way out. Beyond the gate a woman next to a battered VW on the side of the highway was selling "A-Bomb T-Shirts" for five bucks. I smiled at her, rolled on the gas, and shifted into second. In my mirror Stallion Gate shimmered in heat waves and grew small. Soon it was out of sight.

IRON BUTT MAGAZINE – OCTOBER 2010

Why You Ride

PHOTO CREDIT: MATT WATKINS

Riders on the Black Rock Desert near Gerlach, Nevada

Years ago Joe Mandeville, then the president of the Southern California Motorcycle Association, asked me to be the keynote speaker at the club's annual banquet in Los Angeles. The invitation seemed innocent enough; it wasn't. I lived in D.C., approximately nine light-years from L.A. The banquet would take place on February 21. Have you ridden across the country in February? It can rearrange your soul.

So the rational move would be to hop on the giant silver bird, right? I couldn't do that. The summons wasn't coming from Betty Boop of SCMA's social committee. No, this was Mandeville's idea, a man who once rode 106,000 miles in six months. If a legend like Mandeville is buying your dinner, you'll arrive on a bike. Period.

I could have had a clean, weather-free shot all the way to southern California. Anything is possible. But we all know that wasn't in the cards. To avoid some really treacherous winter storms, I ducked down into Mexico, where different challenges in a different language lurked. I've had some nail-biting rides in my life, but this one was harder than trigonometry. A cross-country trip that might have taken four days had instead eaten two weeks. I had slammed into the teeth of El Niño, who seemed bent on dumping cubic miles of the Pacific Ocean onto an already soaked, gasping California.

Still, I had some time to kill, so I rode up to Geyserville, a small town north of San Francisco, to visit friends. It rained all day every day, and then it *really* began to come down. On the morning I was scheduled to head back south I checked the Weather Channel. Not far from me the town of Rio Nido had just slid into the Russian River along with a mountain of mud. The main highway south through Petaluma was beneath two feet of water. Minor roads had disappeared.

I looked at my friends. "I think I can make it." They stared back at me wordlessly. So I began to pack up, trying not to worry about 40 mph winds and rain sluicing down at an inch an hour. But I wasn't going anywhere. The bike had better sense than I did and wouldn't start.

I sat down and tried to reboot my brain. I kept asking myself the same questions: "Why are you doing this stupid shit? Are you insane? Have you abandoned all reason?"

The truth was that I simply didn't know. I'd never thought about these things before, not with any kind of precision or rigor. Now I was stuck in Geyserville with almost nothing to do except reflect on a life devoted in large part to perverse, destructive behavior. Most friends of mine didn't act so irrationally. Why did I? When the rains briefly relented two days later, I motored south. I had arrived at an answer. It wasn't what I'd wanted or expected, but at least I knew. It became the subject of my speech to the SCMA that year.

If you want to find out why people ride bikes, first look at the people who *don't* ride them. That would be 98 percent of the motorists in this country. What do they know that you don't? Well, for starters, when they look at a motorcycle, they don't see a shiny, mechanical horse that might be fun to take for a lope in the park. No, they see a single-track vehicle, inherently unstable except at lethal speeds, that will do whatever it takes to topple onto its side at the first opportunity. They don't see a steed that is a passport to the open road; they see a rattlesnake, a scorpion, or a black widow, all patently dangerous objects that even dull children know to avoid. You may be inclined to write foolish verse in praise of your beloved, but who writes poetry about poisonous reptiles? Not normal people, that's who.

Then there's this icing on the cake: At some point in your life when you bought a bike, you were embarrassed or ashamed even to bring it home. You know it's true. Your mother would have passed out at the thought, right before your father came at you with his belt. You couldn't admit the idiotic thing you'd done, so you squirreled it away in a friend's garage. Yes, you did. This is exactly why Adam and Eve were booted out of the garden. Like them, you abused the trust of those who cared most about you, breached an agreement, and hid your sin. It would have been better if you'd come home with a 7th Avenue whore. At least she wouldn't be trying to kill you.

All right, if 98 percent of the population harbors a well-grounded, primal terror of bikes and your loved ones begin to shudder, kneel, and make the sign of the cross when they discover your secret shame, can we at least agree that they're the normal ones in this crowd and that you're not? And if we can't, then I'm moving on anyway, because you're not only abnormal, you're not following this train of thought very well.

Does it matter how you got this way? It might. A century ago the nature-versus-nurture controversy was in full swing: Does the little Dillinger boy want to ride because he saw Uncle Waylon on a Harley (nurture) or because his brain is hard-wired to rob banks (nature)? In recent years neuroscientists and geneticists have been winning this battle, which made the Human Genome Project such a hot topic. From 1990 to 2003 they unraveled the human DNA sequence, gene by gene, about 25,000 of them. The goal is to find out once and for all what really makes us tick.

Their analysis is far from complete, but I predicted how part of it would end in an article I wrote in the spring of 1992: "Before they are through, they will inevitably find the motorcycle gene. It's the molecule that will be found near the bottom of the DNA ladder, the one that's always fighting with its neighbors."

And when they run it down, we'll see that Uncle Waylon and his Harley had nothing to do with young Johnny Dillinger's depravity. The kid had a defective gene. He literally could not help himself. He was born to rob banks, and so he did. Genetic compulsions produce some of our most primitive responses, what scientists call the four Fs: feeding, fleeing, fighting, and mating. You don't think about it, you just do it. Pondering choices for too long in the jungle can get you killed.

I referred to it as a "motorcycle" gene, but it's really a gene that produces rebellious, anti-social, and not infrequently criminal behavior. All societies have methods of controlling defiant people through psychiatric intervention, waterboarding, federal prison, and so on. But a cheap, effective way of modifying behavior (short of outright surgery) is merely to co-opt it before it becomes intractable: Give the offender a motorcycle license.

At first blush this might appear merely to introduce yet another violent twist into the debate, but its genius is that it diverts a genetic drive to wreak havoc into what we call with a wink a "socially acceptable activity." The rebel with the malignant gene will be riding a motorcycle — perhaps not too skillfully or for too long — instead of robbing widows, selling methamphetamine at the playground, or running for president.

You may recoil from these thoughts, but by standards commonly used to judge the validity of an argument, it passes every test: 1) It conforms with how we know the world works and 2) It isn't internally inconsistent. Look no further than a biker cult classic, *The Wild One*. The leader of the Black Rebels Motorcycle Club is asked, "What're you rebelling against, Johnny?" He replies, "Whaddya got?" It didn't matter; Johnny would rebel against anything. He didn't know why, but we do.

IRON BUTT MAGAZINE – AUGUST 2011

The Curtain

PHOTO CREDIT: THE AUTHOR

Snowed in for two days in the middle of August, Browning, Montana

A year ago in this magazine I wrote a column about why people ride motorcycles. They don't do it to experience the freedom of the road, to feel the wind in their hair, to become one with the travel sprite, or to reconnect with an ancestral horseman. No. They ride because they're insane.

I contend that it is genetic damage — a point still in dispute in scientific circles, but one borne out by my experience — that causes otherwise normal people to act abnormally. In essence they have inherited a recessive gene that produces rebellious, antisocial behavior. You may be inclined to quibble about some of these characterizations, but this much is absolutely clear: Normal people won't go near a motorcycle. Therefore, if you ride a bike, you are deformed by definition. I wish it were otherwise; it is not.

There is another side, equally enigmatic, to this coin. I first saw it expressed by Beau Allen Pacheco in a column in *Rider* magazine more than 20 years ago: Sooner or later, Pacheco wrote, everyone stops riding. It could be anything that does it — the cop is drawing a chalk outline around your body, you're spending more money in emergency rooms than in gas stations, your Gold Wing Road Riders Association uniform is eight sizes too small, or your ego can't take one more Sunday of you being the slowest slug in the group ride. The possibilities, each worse than the last, are infinite.

Here we confront a dilemma, do we not? If you have a genetic compulsion to ride (that activity being a socially acceptable alternative to your otherwise marauding disposition), what counterforce can be sufficiently powerful to overcome it? You will not be surprised to find that I have a theory about that as well. In brief, you stop riding because you have run out of your allotment of bad days.

What is a "bad day," you might ask? Trust me: Like the presence of pornography on the desk of a Supreme Court justice, you'll know it when you see it. Fighting ice and sleet at night on a mountain road; three tire punctures before noon; a failed BMW driveshaft requiring a two-day tow to the nearest dealer; losing a receipt in the last hour of a five-day rally, dropping you from 3rd place to 38th. When even beer and bourbon don't work before bedtime, you've had a bad day.

Admittedly, this is a subjective way to determine a day's status. Mathematical precision is lacking. I thus once spent a year factoring the variables that can influence a day's ride into a complex formula that produced an answer I called a "Fun Unit" (or FU).* It is a number between 0 and 10 — zero being unimaginable disaster and 10 being unattainable perfection. You can set the "bad day" FU score at a level where you think best. For me, anything below 5.0 is a day I should have spent at the library.

So now you can measure a bad day, either subjectively with emotional bias or objectively with a quadratic equation. If I've spent hours slogging through a sleeting crosswind in sub-freezing temperatures on an icy mud track through a backwater landfill in New Jersey the day after my girlfriend threw me under the bus, I could be looking at an FU = 2.3, a grim day by anyone's definition. If I'd had 50 bad days remaining in my allotment bag that morning, I have but 49 at sundown.

The trouble with all this is that no one knows how many bad days he or she is born with. In that sense, they're like time and money. It doesn't matter what you've spent; all that counts is how much you have left. And with bad days, we never know. We just know when they're gone.

Perhaps there is a ray of sunshine here. Wouldn't it be possible to avoid even getting on the bike when, for example, every weather sign is pointing to disaster? And in that vein in December 1999 *Motorcycle Consumer News* published a column by Brenda Bates arguing that motorcyclists possess "rider's intuition" or a "gut instinct" that tells them when they should stay off the bike. So if the weather reports are predicting hail, typhoon winds, and black ice and your rider's intuition is screaming at you to stay in bed, then you should be able to avoid a bad day simply by not riding, yes?

No, for two reasons. First, the rebel gene that puts you on the bike to begin with is going to urge you, "Sure, it looks bad, but you're the king of the road. You can make it." Second, when Bates reluctantly admitted that the concept of rider intuition was not an "exact science," she was at least correct there. It isn't science at all. It's laughable nonsense. No one, not even an astronomer, can predict the future.

If you're beginning to feel the oppressive cloud of Calvinistic predestination descending on you right now, you're not alone. But although you won't be able to avoid a bad day even if you can see one coming, it may yet be possible to minimize the worst case by taking some simple precautions. The very first tip in the Iron Butt Archive of Wisdom is "Know your limits." The 12th tip is "Know when to stop." Yes, you'll very likely get some arguments from the rebel gene here and there, but at least give these ideas a try. They can't hurt and may actually help.

Here are a few other suggestions that may keep the wolf from the door. They are merely variants on the usual underlying theme, that being you start with a bag full of luck and an empty bag of experience, The goal is to fill up the bag of experience before you empty the bag of luck:

1. Wear the right clothes. Years ago I ran across a guy on the Kaibab plateau in northern Arizona. Fierce, black clouds covered the horizons from pole to pole. He had no rain suit. Within an hour, irrespective of the direction he

might take, hypothermia would be his co-pilot. And anyone riding in any season in North America without at least an electric vest is just begging for a bad day.

2. Learn how to understand weather patterns. It is occasionally possible to outmaneuver a storm. Local TV stations are far better guides here than the worthless, disaster-hyping Weather Channel.

3. Learn routine maintenance and do it. You may not be able to troubleshoot a failed R80 diode board on the side of the road, but you should at least be able to plug a tire.

4. Use the right tool. Take a dirt bike on a forest trail and a Gold Wing on I-70, not the other way around. This would seem self-evident. Apparently it is not.

5. Never eat at a place called Mom's.

That's it, my little monsters. It's not even rocket psychiatry. Avoid a string of bad days, maybe win a rally or a mileage contest, become rich and famous along the way, and you can be the guest columnist in this space next year. I need a rest anyway. I feel a bad day coming on.

* See, *Tchebycheff and Me*, page 38.

When Memory Fades

(L-R) The author and Ed Culberson in Orlando, Florida, at the start of Amigo's last ride

This bike, an '81 BMW R80G/S, feels as old and tired as I do. The huge tank is battered and touched up with paint that is laughably mismatched. A thick rubber band circles the instrument cluster, squeezing everything together. Cracked saddlebags let in the rain. It is a five-stroke engine, the last one being Faith.

I am taking this bike on its last ride. Of a half-million or more BMWs produced in 70 years, few are more famous than this one. *Amigo* is painted on the sides of the tank. What was once bold color is now pastel and fading, as paint will do after 267,000 miles.

But in 12 brutal days in February 1986 this motorcycle slogged out of a jungle and into immortality.

Its owner, Ed Culberson, is a legend in BMW circles. A retired military officer, explorer, writer, and MSF Chief Instructor whose students included Peace Corps volunteers, he is also the kindest, most gracious man one could meet. But privately, in his younger days, he was by his own admission obsessed: He wanted to ride *Amigo* the length of the Pan-American Highway, from Alaska to the bottom of South America, including the nearly impenetrable jungle between Panama and Colombia — the infamous Darien Gap.

The stretch from the Yukon to Panama was easy. But the road stopped there. Culberson stared at a green wall to the south. His first assault on the Darien ended in failure. The following year, when the rains abated in early 1986, he made it, pushing the bike through a 67-mile path he cut with a machete, canoeing across rivers, and ultimately emerging in

Colombia after nearly two weeks of unimaginable hardship. Then he continued south until the road stopped again. He stood in Tierra del Fuego; to the south, across the Straits of Magellan, lay Antarctica.

It had taken two years, but *Amigo* was the first vehicle ever to have traveled the western hemisphere nearly from pole to pole. The incredible story of triumph over monumentally adverse conditions is related in Culberson's 1991 book, *Obsessions Die Hard*.

Now Ed himself is dying. The hand that throttled a motorcycle through jungle mud is weak, the victim of Lou Gehrig's disease. He will never sit on his bike again. I volunteer to take it from Ed's home in Florida to the *Rider* rally in Richmond, Kentucky. There a BMW company transport truck will take it to Westerville, Ohio. It is going into the AMA museum, to sit for a year with its equals. Few are.

I tell Ed what an honor it is to ride his bike as he hands me the key. Some last photos are taken. His daughter helps him into the car and we wave goodbye. He and his bike, together for so long and through so much, part. I ride north.

This poor motor will look out of place in the sea of gleaming Wings with their winking lights and neon glow on the rally grounds of Richmond. An ocean of Armor All will never clean the bike; the jungle did its work well and permanently. But in the Westerville museum each dent and tinge of rust will be a valorous badge of the highest distinction.

Near Nancy, Kentucky, the sun is not cooperating. I want to see it drop below the horizon at the end of a limitless stretch of straight highway. And I want to take a photo with a telephoto lens of the motorcycle heading into that setting sun, to make it look like a yellow basketball a yard from my nose. But this is hilly country, there are late afternoon clouds, and I give up. The picture I never capture of *Amigo* that afternoon still remains as clear to me as any Kodak moment I ever had.

The sun disappears. In the east, a few degrees above the horizon, a full, bright orange moon is rising. It is perfect, this planetary Zen, with one body vanishing and another appearing in a galactic juggling act. Ed is dying, his daughter marries; *Amigo* goes into a museum and another BMW rolls off the Berlin assembly line; now the sky darkens and tomorrow there is light anew.

In time everything will fade, like the paint on the tank. Ed and those of us who had the privilege of knowing him will be no more. Maybe then *Amigo* will be forgotten. But I hope not.

SUMMIT POINT RACETRACK MAGAZINE – APRIL 1988

How I Spent My Summer Vacation

PHOTO CREDIT: THE AUTHOR

Westbound from Escalante, Utah

When I was young and stupid, I would watch *Then Came Bronson* and imagine a motorcycle's headlight beam cutting a knife-like swath along the inky blackness of a curving forest road. Later, when I began to realize that animals the size of Gorgon the Defiler inhabited those forests, I decided that riding a bike at night was a guaranteed ticket to the nearest rehabilitation hospital. Consequently, I have never been much known in the trade as a Long-Distance Man. For the last 20 years, my idea of a fairly serious motorcycle junket has been a round trip to the Safeway a mile away for a pack of cigarettes.

Given that background, let us turn back the clock one year. We are reading about the adventures of one Jeff Brody, the touring columnist of the BMW Motorcycle Owners of America *News*, a club magazine devoted to uplifting the spirits of those who, having bought one of the Legendary Motorcycles of Germany (as the ads modestly proclaim), are now having trouble making payment on the second mortgage that was required to buy the damned bike in the first place.

Brody's reputation is that of a guy who lives on a bike, averaging over 40,000 miles of two-wheeled travel each year. I note that in his current column he has mentioned in passing that he had set a solo record by touching the 48 contiguous states in 11 days, 7 hours, 15 minutes. That record intrigued me. After studying a road atlas for a few hours, I concluded that he must have been averaging about 750 miles per day. That, I thought, safely put any thoughts about such a trip for me firmly out of the question: At that point in my life, the longest trip I had ever made in a single day was just over 450 rib-cracking miles, followed immediately by critical-care unit therapy off and on for the next six months.

But the idea kept rattling around in the back of my head like a BB. Could I do something like that? Wasn't I at age 47 just a little beyond my sell-by date? As the spring weather kicked in, I sold my rusted-out but relatively reliable 650cc BMW and bought a new 750cc bike that was BMW's latest answer to the Japanese rice-grinders, a sports rider's dream.

June is always a bad month to try to invade something large. Ask Napoleon. Ask Hitler. Ask me. What Brody had done, I decided, could be replicated by any idiot and nobody was a better idiot than was I. On an overcast morning in early June, I set out to blow Brody away in 11 days flat, a trip that would require averaging 775 miles per day. I prepared for my adventure with a three-day ride of 500 total miles, one that left me only partially paralyzed. The pain would go away, I thought. After leaving my house in northwest Washington, D.C., I had bagged both Maryland and Virginia in under 10 minutes. At that rate I would be home before dark.

There's no point in belaboring this ill-conceived disaster. If you could make a wrong move in the first days of a big ride, I made it. Three days after leaving home I was back in it, accompanied by cervical nerve problems of the sell-this-bike kind. It was a beautiful thing, that K75S, but it was killing my neck.

When I got back into the real world, the first thing I did was write an article about my ignominious defeat and send it to the MOA *News*. It was a labor of self-mockery and denigration titled "Tell Jeff Brody to Stop Worrying: His 48 State Record Is Safe From Me." A week later I tried to drive up to Thurmont, Maryland, to visit a BMW bike campout, but my neck blew up again. This was getting tedious. Either that bike had to go or I would be spending the last 20 years of my life in a wheelchair. A few weeks later I sold the traitor and bought yet another BMW, a mechanical duplicate of the bike that had tried to put me into a neck brace, but this time outfitted in a true touring style.

By August I was looking at the maps again. Then my father died. That *really* pissed me off. I decided that I needed to get away.

First I went to the Bahamas and snorkeled for sharks. When I got back home, I was still wired. After sitting around the office for a few days, I looked at the weather map. It was Thursday, August 27, 1987, and there wasn't a cloud anywhere in the entire country. This was too good to pass up. I told my secretary that I was going to lunch and that I'd be back on the day after Labor Day. I went home and packed up the bike again. That night at 10 p.m. I pulled the bike out of the drive-way in the presence of two witnesses. "OK, Brody," I muttered, "watch this." I shot out toward I-66, hooked a left onto I-81 and stopped for a few minutes for a buns break. The proposed schedule was simplicity itself: 85 miles on the bike, pause 10 minutes, and ride again until the low fuel light would come on, generally in another 85 miles or so. Average 32 miles per hour, 24 hours per day. Don't stop to talk to anyone, don't take detours, and don't take pictures of anything but the "Welcome to X" state boundary marker.

This was going to be travel as if painting by number. Stay on the route, watch the printout to make sure you're not behind, don't look at anything except where you're going. Day one. Check. Maybe it's not a lot of fun, but it's progress. Day two. Check. There's a goal up the road, Bobby. Get going.

On the third day I was again up well before dawn and on the road. Oklahoma greeted me with a pothole that almost ripped off the right side of the bike. The road then went north along the eastern border of the state. I hooked into Missouri off the Oklahoma interstate, then came to the Kansas border about two minutes later. This wasn't a part of the trip that I was looking forward to. There isn't anything to see in Kansas and there's always a wretched southerly wind to fight through. By the time I made Oakley in west-central Kansas in mid-evening, I was convinced that the entire state had been hammered with a neutron bomb. I stopped, drank a few beers, changed oil, and walked straight into a wall looking for the shower. With the exception of two medicinal Tequila Sunrises that I prescribed for myself in Reno two days later, it was the last alcohol I would have on the trip: I was becoming dangerously stupid.

On the fourth day I began to air the bike out. Normally I don't drive much above 75 mph but now that I was in true Cowboyland, anything under 100 mph seemed appropriate. After clipping the corner of Nebraska and almost running out of gas, I steamed down the eastern border of Colorado on U.S. 385 averaging about 85 mph, jogged over to Limon on the interstate, and then rocketed down Colorado 71 at 90-plus mph. In 76 miles of that road, there is but a single intersection.

An hour later the Rockies came into view, blocked out the sun, and waited patiently while I took a very small picture. One day, I thought, these will erode into the sea. I began to feel comfortable for the first time, to realize my actual place in the firmament: a little carbon speck crawling around on a little metal speck in an empty universe. In a few hours I was through La Veta and Wolf Creek passes, past Durango, circling Four Corners at dusk, and into Blanding, Utah, at nightfall. I sat in the motel with some Pringles and looked at the maps. With luck I would be spending the next night in Susanville, California, the halfway point.

On Utah 95 and 24, I sliced north and west toward Delta, the ultimate desert outpost in west-central Utah. I triple-dosed on No. 15 sun block, injected another half-quart of Dr Pepper, and at just past noon I shot west toward Reno, 450 miles away. An hour later, three miles short of the Nevada border, my back tire went flat. I'd never fixed a flat on any vehicle in my entire life.

U.S. 12 in Idaho, one of America's most spectacular highways

You cannot find anywhere in the continental United States that is farther away from anything than where I was. For 15 minutes I just sat down in the sand by the side of the empty road and looked at the sky. It finally occurred to me that the problem would probably not fix itself. I managed to plug the tubeless tire and shoot some compressed air into it. I limped toward Ely. No tires available. I called the nearest BMW dealer, in Reno, and told them that I'd be in the next morning. As I left the edge of town, I saw a sign: "U.S. 50 — The Loneliest Road in America."

It may be lonely out there, and it was, but it was the most haunting day of the trip. The scenery was magnificent beyond any words and the tension was as much as I ever want to feel. But I hit Reno without further incident, got a good night's sleep for the first time on the trip, and had the tire fixed easily the following morning. "That's it," I mumbled to myself, swinging onto the bike and heading for California. "It's all downhill from here. If that didn't grind me down, nothing will."

And nothing did. I got back into my driveway five-and-one-half days later on Sunday evening. A small "Welcome Home" party was already underway. It would have been my old man's 77th birthday.

EPILOGUE

I slept in on Labor Day. When I awoke, I asked Susan to see if the bike was still in the driveway. I thought that at dawn, out of sheer habit, it might have driven off by itself. It hadn't moved.

The next day I sent a telegram to Jeff Brody:

NEW 48 STATE SOLO RECORD:
10 DAYS 21 HOURS 37 MINUTES.
DETAILS TO FOLLOW.

Nearly three weeks passed in silence. Then I got a postcard from Brody:

"Dear Robert: I hope you enjoyed your
trip. The record is 10 days 15 hours for a
non-documented tour, though. My record
lasted a month and was broken by a 70-plus-
year-old man, Ron Chapman. His claim
is not documented, though. If you have
documentation of the 48-state nature of your
trip, you at least beat me."

Slowly I sat down. Then I laughed. It was just too much. After 8,400 miles through the winds of Hell was my prize to be not immortality itself but an all-expense-paid vacation for two in Beirut? "Oh, yes," I smiled, "this is poetic justice of the rarest and most horrible sort."

I took out the maps again, looked at my mistakes, considered the possibilities for a spring assault. Ten days. Ten days. It wouldn't be that bad. Ten days, easy. But then I thought of the Japanese woman I had seen when I was 15 years old, laboring up Fuji on a pilgrimage, looking as if she were carrying the weight of a universe on her arched back.

Sometimes, even now and usually when I am not expecting it, my memory will drift to a dim scene of a headlight in the Nevada twilight, miles away, coming toward me. It will be a bike, I know. Even at a high closing speed, we will not meet for at least a minute. In those moments I would think, "And so we shall meet at last, Señor Brody."

A Heavy Burden

The author at the U.S. Capitol

Some people can disagree without being disagreeable. I can't. My opinions tend to be inflexible. If you don't share them, you might think of persuading me through debate and philosophical discourse. I'd rather burn down your house.

Hence, it was with some consternation that I read Robin Boltz' spirited defense of mandatory helmet laws in the December 2007 issue of *On the Level*. Part of me thought mutual benefits might be attained were I modestly to point out to Robin the 59 errors of logic, epidemiology, political science, bioethics, regression analysis, sociology, Ohm's Law, metaphysics, and stoichiometry that riddled her monograph. Another part of me simply wanted to head to her home with a can of gasoline.

But she and I go way back. And you can't find more saintly people than Robin and her much-beloved husband Gordan, former president-for-life of this club. Maybe a torch and five gallons of fuel weren't the answers this time. A few glasses of pinot grigio calmed me down. I dialed her number. She picked up immediately, convincing me that she didn't have caller ID.

"Robin," I began, "I have in my hand this . . . this, *thing* you've written. Let me see if I follow your proposition: Society wastes money treating the head injuries of motorcyclists who weren't wearing helmets; helmets could have prevented (or lessened the extent of) the injuries; therefore society has the right to force motorcyclists to wear helmets. Is that it?"

"That's it," she agreed.

"With all due respect I disagree. Society has no right whatsoever to compel me to do anything unless my behavior will cause harm to others, and economic harm is never a sufficient warrant. See John Stuart Mill's essay, *On Liberty*, published in 1859. Wearing a helmet might make me healthier, happier, and safer. I don't care. It might be wise, a fashion statement, and financially prudent. Again, I don't care. In matters of this sort I ask one thing and one thing only of the government: Leave me the hell alone. As Mills wrote, 'Over himself, over his own body and mind, the individual is sovereign.' Have I thus convinced you by the onslaught of unassailable reason to recant your flawed views and abandon that poxed, Marxist mentality forthwith?"

"No," she laughed.

Stymied, and not for the first time, I was left with no recourse but to provide fair warning to my errant friend. "Robin, as your attorney, I advise you to buy some fire insurance."

Nearly 20 years ago Robin's identical arguments were used by the State of Maryland in an attempt to force bikers to procure catastrophic medical insurance. "We're spending millions to treat these injured bikers," the governor's spokesmen said. "They won't wear helmets. And helmets could save them."

We pointed out that Maryland was spending 50 times more to treat head injuries sustained by car crash victims than it expended on motorcyclists. Would there be, we asked, a comparable proposal to compel automobile operators and passengers to wear helmets and carry massive levels of medical insurance? Of course not. The state preferred to focus solely on irrational bikers, who represented but two percent of vehicular traffic.

We learned something about real-world politics in the insurance war, something they hadn't taught us in seventh-grade civics. It isn't really about the money; it's about the power to bend some poor sucker to your will. It's called the tyranny of the majority: We outnumber you, so you'll do what's good for yourself or we'll fine you, take away your property, or throw your ignorant ass into jail.

To promote a justifiably worthy end — insert a *cause du jour* here such as second-hand smoke, trans-fats, biofuels, global warming, universal health care, or helmets — any means and any evidence will suffice. Only one question arises: Do I have the votes to shove it down the opposition's throat? I'll make up scientific studies; I'll demonize my foes and call them irresponsible and reckless burdens on society; I will appeal to prejudice of any sort by the use of logical fallacies without number and rhetorical misdirection without end.

But it's good for you, they tell me. We know best, they say. I cannot describe the effect such words have upon me from the lips of Hillary Clinton or George Bush. I'd rather hear from Louis Brandeis: "Experience should teach us to be most on our guard to protect liberty when the government's purposes are beneficial. The greatest dangers to liberty lurk in insidious encroachment by men of zeal, well meaning but without understanding."

Amen. And given that, would Brandeis even be surprised to learn that the administrator of the National Highway Transportation Safety Administration is never an engineer or accident investigator or lawyer or architect or urban planner or skillful bureaucrat? No, the agency is always run by someone trained as an emergency-room physician. Why? Because trauma doctors see a lot of car crashes, and to a man with a hammer, the whole world looks like a nail. Stop the activity and you stop the risk. Stop the risk and you stop the injuries. QED.

Once you wave goodbye to Mills and start down the road toward the goal of a risk-free society, there is no logical stopping point. That's why my libertarian friends and I argue so desperately and become so excited so quickly. We've seen what a nanny state can do when it moves into high gear, with the inevitable result of its meddling being to deprive us of life, liberty, and the pursuit of happiness. When I was in Grant Junior High School, Miss Kelley told me that they couldn't do that.

But they can. I remember the enactment of the first seatbelt law. Even then I knew it was the beginning of the end. *How many unbelted passengers have been ejected from cars and slammed into innocent pedestrians,* I wondered idly. As I did, Mills spun in his grave. I used to smoke cigarettes in airplanes. Then I'd puff in the back of the plane. Then just in the terminal. Then outside the terminal. Fifteen years ago in San Francisco a cop nearly arrested me for smoking *outside* the terminal. I've offered for as long as I can recall to buy dinner for anyone who can show me an unbiased study merely tending to prove that second-hand smoke has ever harmed anyone. I haven't paid up yet.

We're beyond that now. In the game of political poker FDR anted with Social Security and a New Deal; Johnson called with Medicare and a Great Society; Nixon raised with OSHA, EPA, and adopted the economic theories of John Maynard Keynes, a Fabian socialist; Bush shoved in all his chips with drug benefits for rich geezers and a war that his great-grandchildren will be paying for. Who's going to win this pot? Republican? Democrat? Not me.

> *The fox's teeth are in the bunny*
> *And nothing can remove them, honey.*

I stand on the shore, watching a ship that sailed long ago. When they figure out that I can never be absolutely safe on the bike, they'll crush that too for my own good. In the meantime I'll console myself with Gavin Ewart's poems about foxes and bunnies. And a can of gasoline.

The Master

Another day at the office for Barbara Williams

Like a lot of you guys, I got into motorcycling to make some real money, improve my social standing, and meet lots of women. The first two goals haven't worked out too well so far, but at least I've met a woman. And although she isn't actual dating material — being already married with four kids — in one respect she's turned out to be better than a girlfriend: She's my mechanic.

Barbara Williams isn't just any mechanic, either. She's one of the long-ball hitters in the shop at BMW of Daytona, the place that recently has been selling more bikes than any other BMW dealership in the country. Even better, she has a master's certification from BMW Motorrad, an achievement that is shared by just 79 other mechanics in North America. Those other wrenches, by the way, all are men.

Like many matches made in heaven, the relationship between my wrench and me was one of love at first sight: I am drawn to people who know more about the insides of BMW bikes than I do and she was attracted to my license plate — 81067F — the numbers representing her birth date and the "F" obviously signifying her gender. This, I thought, is too good to be true.

If you've got the brains of a wart, you know that a happy mechanic is more valuable than a soul mate whose father owns a liquor store, so I hustled down to the Department of Motor Vehicles and tried to have the plate reassigned to Barbara's bike.

"Can do?" I begged in my most plaintive voice.

"No can do," the humorless clerk replied.

Still, I picked up some points for making the attempt. Things, especially good things, often take time to develop.

No one knows that better than Mrs. Williams. She and husband Ted ("Not the Red Sox player," she notes) married young and settled on the New Jersey shore. While they were on vacation in Florida during Bike Week in 1992, a vicious storm was busy pounding their house up north. It was a message from Mother Nature that the Williams couldn't ignore. They and their kid returned to New Jersey long enough to quit jobs and school, sell what was left of the house, pack the truck to the gills, kiss New Jersey goodbye for good, and head back down I-95 to the Sunshine State.

No job was waiting for either Barbara or Ted, but within 18 hours of crossing the Florida line, they had settled into a house in Edgewater, just south of Daytona. It is a town that had previously been famous only as the hunting grounds of Aileen Wuornos, America's most prolific female serial killer.

She and Ted soon discovered two inescapable facts about the Florida economy: 1) people will work for peanuts there because they can't stand the thought of spending another winter in Jersey City; and 2) employers know that. Barbara eventually found a position as a data-entry clerk at an auction yard in the northwest suburbs of Daytona, watching her salary climb over the course of eight years from not much to a little more than not much. Her depression was growing faster than her wages.

"I had a job," she said. "But I needed a career."

On the way to work in the morning she would drive past the American Motorcycle Institute, a school for training motorcycle and watercraft mechanics. Ted had taught her to ride when she was 30, but although she'd always liked bikes and bikers, she had never thought about motorcycles as anything but a hobby. Now she began to hear the siren call of opportunity. *Why not?* she thought. Sure, she couldn't imagine ever having to wrestle with a bike on the floor of the garage in a dealership, but if she graduated, she conceivably might find a job as a service writer or a parts specialist.

Eleven years earlier a storm had altered the Williams' lives. Now a metaphorical storm was kicking up the surf again. Barbara quit her job, cashed in her savings from a retirement plan, qualified for a student loan, and entered AMI in the spring of 2003. Thousands of students had preceded her in the school's 30-plus-year history, betting their futures just as Barbara would do.

It is a relentless, grueling regimen. The curriculum lasts 20 weeks, five days a week, from 8:00 in the morning to 5:00 in the afternoon. Attendance is taken four times a day, just as they do in well-run penitentiaries. Start missing classes and you'll be on the street before you can name the parts of a Mikuni carburetor. The only thing that will get you pounded more quickly is taking a swing at an instructor, again just like the Big House.

The first 10 weeks are devoted to motorcycles in general, their care, feeding, and tickling. You study drive shafts, gearboxes, turn-signal switches, and needle jets. You stick spokes on wheels and try to make them turn without a wobble. You adjust valves, test starter motors, sniff for emissions, bleed brakes, and drop engine blocks on your toes. Every eight minutes, it seems, the instructor is asking you another question you don't know how to answer. During lunch you study books and handouts and diagrams and countless parts. At the end of the day, if you're not worn out, you've been sleeping. And they won't let you sleep.

If you make if through the first half of the course — 20 percent don't — the final 10 weeks are principally devoted to studying the sort of bike that brought you to the school in the first place: Harley-Davidson (the overwhelming majority), BMW, Ducati, or Japanese marques. Barbara had originally signed up for H-D but switched over to BMW, sensing a better market opportunity down the road. In Daytona you can't swing a cat without hitting a guy who can take apart a Panhead with one hand and crack open another Bud with the other.

It was a good choice. While many of her classmates were studying surf bunnies at the beach, Barbara spent nights and weekends staring at a mountain of BMW technical bulletins. In a righteous world this sort of devotion rarely pays off, but for our heroine her reach was just long enough to grab the brass ring. In September 2003 she graduated with honors (a grade point average above 3.50), was second in her class, and the following day began work as an entry-level mechanic at Bill Peretti's BMW of Daytona franchise.

Her training hasn't stopped. She returned to AMI, one of the locations where BMW holds advanced training, for additional certification in electrics. In December 2005 she began training for the master's level. They don't hold this course often, so it's difficult even to be accepted. But Barbara's supervisor, shop manager Lee Florin, had been calling AMI every day to check on openings. She was just one of eight mechanics to start and, when the dust settled, was the only one who had successfully completed all the requirements of the course.

The Daytona Beach *News-Journal* did a front-page story about the local "Motorcycle Mama" who'd missed the graduation party in her honor because she was taking care of her own kid and the three foster children that she and Ted had taken in. The reporter herself seemed perplexed that a mere woman could cope with the mysteries of fuel injection and anti-lock brakes. But for Barbara it was just another day at the office. "If you can put together a Barbie doll house, you can put together anything."

Her recent notoriety aside, life has pretty much returned to normal around the bike lifts and oil drums in the Daytona dealership. Mark Sanchez, a fellow wrench who received his master's certification a couple of years ago, says that Barbara is "just one of the guys." She is, after all, the one who keeps all the bikes in the Ocala Police Department on the highway.

Still, vestiges of male chauvinism remain, as evidenced by a telephone call that Barbara recently took.

"The customer didn't want to talk to me," she recalls with a smile. "He'd talk to Mark or Lee but not to me. No problem."

It may seem a bit coarse to admit it, but I sincerely applaud this sort of attitude. Sure, it's rude and idiotic, but the less time Barbara has to spend dealing with guys mired like this in the 12th century, the more time she'll have to spend on my poor beaters. And Lord knows they need the best help they can find.

RIDER – AUGUST 1994

The Devil's Sign

And it just keeps getting harder…

It's hard to imagine what sort of Earth Day celebration might have happened this year at Morenci, Arizona. For 75 years, beginning in the 1860s, miners hacked away underground for copper, gold, and miscellaneous ores that don't even have names. Then they got serious. The mine is now an open sore two miles across and 2,000 feet deep from which a quarter-million tons of ore are ripped *every day*. The hole that is left when 23 billion tons of rock disappear is most impressive. Perhaps if one could get closer to the bottom of the pit, one might see the gateway to Hell.

If there is a river in the area, it drains the Earth's tears.

New Mexico 53 is as old a road as you can find, older than time, two years older than God. It was already ancient when Coronado trekked along it 450 years ago on the most malicious wild-goose chase in recorded history. The Zuni have used it, as lawyers say, "until the memory of man runneth not to the contrary." I had been westbound on it out of Grants for more than an hour when I bumped into Arizona and came to a T a few miles later. Relatively indifferent as to direction on this exquisite early May afternoon, but not wanting to recover I-40 to the north, I turned left and south to Springerville and gas. In the desert, where I seem to spend a disproportionate part of my motorcycle life, it's always a good idea to fill up where possible. The map showed only one intersection in the next 100 miles.

During the break I switched state maps to find out where I was going. Ah. A curvy road abutted with orange hash marks, usually a reasonable indication of Rand McNally's idea of sceniosity. As a solo rider, I often make up words to pass the time. I tightened the bike's rubber-band motor two clicks past Lurch Mode and continued south.

When I first saw the sign, I stopped. I am sure that I must have seen something that indicated the road's identification before that point, but I stopped anyway. Long-distance solo riding is pretty much a matter of unconsciousness. A United States route number: 666. It didn't occur to me until two days later that I had never seen a U.S. highway with a number that large. *Six six six?* The number rattled around my subcortex like an anatomical BB. The sound of it was indisputably ugly, but I couldn't place it.

At the town of Alpine, the road began to climb. Had I any doubt about what was coming up, it was dispelled a few moments later when the first of what would become an increasingly hysterical series of warning signs appeared:

CURVES
MOUNTAIN GRADES
NEXT 30 MILES

As promised, the highway began to twist and shout. After a while, the road crews had apparently tired of putting up curve-warning speeds and had defaulted to a single, simple curve-warning sign:

20 MPH
NEXT 12 MILES

Fair warning, the last words out of the auctioneer's mouth just before the gavel falls and you've once again committed to something that you can't afford. The road continued to reach toward the sky, slithering all the way.

The smell of the pine forest was so intense it was almost distracting. I recall passing about 50 different animal-warning signs, including a buffalo crossing, before the hammer dropped again.

PHOTO CREDIT: THE AUTHOR

Sign of the devil

**15 MPH
NEXT 6 MILES**

The corners became tighter. With the thick trees growing right to the edge of the road, any view of oncoming traffic or an informed guess about the curve's true radius was impossible. From corner to corner the trip devolved to slam-and-jam. My right wrist throbbed with the tension.

Over a crest, as the road yanked viciously to the left, the trees disappeared to the right. I whacked both brakes and slid to a halt at a turnout. The horizon, a hazy, magnificent blue, spread out to the south and west, to the very edge of the universe. The altitude had to have exceeded 8,500 feet. For a few minutes I sat at the edge of the road, staring at the endless series of mountain ridges. *A day like this is the payback*, I thought. *For the cold, the rain, the wind. This is Miller time.*

The road descended. At a construction site I talked with one of the crew. They were paving the road with good intentions. He promised that it would straighten out as I got closer to Morenci. There had been just about one curve too many; if you take enough of them on a bike, sooner or later one will bite you. I don't care how good you are.

10 MPH
NEXT 11 MILES

I pulled up to the sign and sagged back in the seat. I'm not much of a mathematician, but I know a linear regression when I see one. If this deterioration continued, the last sign was ordained straight out of a Calvinist nightmare:

0 MPH
FOREVER

Time would stop, the Earth would become infinitely small and infinitely dense, and the Devil and Einstein would walk hand in hand to Nogales for a Corona. A psychotic break was around the next corner. Or the one after that.

For 11 miles I subtracted tenths, one after another. *This was the wrong direction to take this road*, I thought. *I should have come from the south. The more tired I got, the harder the road got. Life's not fair.* And then, as radically as it had begun, the road turned into a country stroll, light, casual, and easy. Cattle, not buffalo, walked along the shoulder; cactus and sage struggled out of the sand. I was back in my world, not His. It was still 666, but purgatory, not Hell.

And then I got to the mine at Morenci.

I sent away recently for the Top 10 Motorcycle Highways video. When it arrived, I popped a beer, sat down in front of the tube, and waited for The Road. It isn't there. There are, it's true, 10 decent motorcycle roads on the tape, but one is missing. Somehow I knew it would be. I've never talked to a single soul who has been on it.

But it's out there, waiting. I swear.

[Postscript: Alas, the designation of the "Beast Highway" succumbed to the combined wills of the governors of Arizona, New Mexico, and Colorado on May 31, 2003. It was renumbered U.S. 491. As a New Mexico highway official explained, "As long as it's not 666 and it's nothing satanic, that's OK."]

Crime and Punishment

Two Lawyers Conversing, by Honoré Daumier (1808-1879)

Earlier this year motorcyclists went into orbit when a judge in Michigan gave 90 days in jail to the operator of a car, driving on a suspended license, who mowed down and killed a motorcyclist. In passing sentence the judge observed, more or less, that the driver probably wasn't at fault because no one can see motorcyclists anyway.

The Third Amendment to the Constitution says, I think, that it is your duty as a citizen to criticize a judicial decision, even though you weren't at the trial, haven't read the court transcript, and aren't entirely clear what legal principles, if any, apply to the case. Thus, in a blink, calls for the judge's banishment from the human race erupted from bikers far and wide. I took a different view, of course, since I live in a bunker.

First, I asked, suppose there had been testimony from reputable scientists that the human eye is deficient when it comes to identifying and judging relatively small, darting objects like bumblebees, curve balls, or sport bikes. The judge could easily have found, based on just that sort of evidence, that there had been no criminal intent on the part of the defendant and the relatively light sentence consequently could have been handed down simply for the suspended license charge.

Second, I asked, does such evidence about the limitations of human eyesight really exist? I stated that I knew a PhD psychologist/statistician, a man with impeccable credentials from NHTSA, AAA, and academia, who would testify honestly that human beings don't see bikes all that well.

We all know that, don't we? Isn't that why we put WATCH FOR MOTORCYCLISTS bumper stickers on our cars? Isn't that why we're taught that we should ride as if we're invisible? The nasty truth is that for all practical purposes, we are. They really can't see us. I wish it weren't so, but the evidence says it is.

Those comments didn't win me any new friends, of course, but I already have enough friends. When a motorcyclist is killed, the reaction of surviving motorcyclists is to form a lynch mob, go after the offending motorist (whether he's been proven to be culpable or not), and string up anyone who's on that killer's side (including, I guess, the judge who failed to sentence the miscreant to life on a rock pile in the first place).

Lynching has fallen into disfavor in recent years, so the fallback position has become the enhancement of existing laws. You see this with the advent of hate crimes. If I burn down the Church of the Quivering Brethren, I have committed the felonious act of arson. If you want to prove that I also didn't like the Brethren — which should be pretty obvious since I just turned their church into a cinder — have you added anything to the case? I contend you have added nothing. You're not meting out justice any longer; you're simply dispensing an additional serving of vengeance.

Now I am acutely aware that revenge is one of the four pillars of criminal law (the others being deterrence, rehabilitation, and incarceration). But revenge for its own sake has a sort of primitive, light-the-torches ring to it. We are a society that strives to make our calls for stinging retribution more subtle. Still, there's a dead biker on the road. It could have been you or me. Let's hammer the bastard who did it before it really *is* you or me.

But we have a problem: Hate-crime classification won't work here. It's difficult to prove that the cager had a malevolent heart and wiped out the biker in consequence thereof. Sure, any of us would happily murder a squid in mid-wheelie or a Neanderthal with straight pipes. But there's no real evidence that motorists in general hate bikers or view them as a despised, untouchable caste.

Suppose then, instead of concentrating on the perpetrator's state of mind, we focus on the status of the victim, to wit, the motorcyclist. We will endeavor to give the rider a special station merely because of who he is. There is precedent for this. Certain actors in the law have a privileged, honored place. When I graduated from law school, my ambition was to become a holder in due course, one of the law's most favored children.

All we lack is a snappy slogan. How about "Kill a Biker, Go to Jail"? It's short, sweet, and menacing. It accomplishes the goal of turning what could have been an innocent accident, or at worst simple negligence, into a criminal act. It doesn't focus on the offender. We don't care anything about the mind of the offender at all, as we surely do with hate crimes. Here we look only at the body on the road. Is it a biker? Yes? Go to jail.

Do you like this development? Motorcyclists in Virginia apparently do. They recently prevailed on their general assembly to pass a variant of the "Kill a Biker, Go to Jail" law. The American Motorcyclist Association, which hasn't been winning much of anything in courtrooms for 10 years, is solidly behind the strategy. Who could possibly be against it?

Well, *moi*, I'm afraid, because the question I posed originally remains unanswered: What if the eyeballs of the average motorist are essentially incapable of seeing motorcyclists? The criminal law is predicated on the existence of *mens rea*, or criminal intent. If Mother Hubbard in her '55 DeSoto, otherwise fit by all applicable standards to operate a car, didn't see Bobby Biker because to her optical system he is the size of a hummingbird, then she couldn't possibly have intended to hurt Bobby, much less kill him. She didn't mean to do anything wrong. She has no guilty mind. But Bobby's dead, and because he was a biker, Mother Hubbard is going to jail.

If you believe in the basic fairness of The System, this sort of law will not look like a sword waiting to cut you in half. You will not see how the worm can turn, because you believe that prosecutors seek nothing but simple justice and that juries are omniscient and that judges dispense only sentences where the punishment fits the crime. I would like to live there in Bunnyland with you, but I don't.

The truth is that prosecutors are ravenous beasts and are interested only in conviction rates. Juries routinely produce verdicts that are nothing if not laughable. Judges may want to do the right thing, but their hands are increasingly tied by mandatory minimum sentences that remove all discretion, which I thought was the *sine qua non* of judging in the first place. Kill a biker, go to jail. Period.

Once we strove for homogeneity. *E Pluribus Unum.* Now we lobby for special interests. Motorcyclists are skillful at that kind of activity, and sometimes — as in the case of high-occupancy vehicle lanes access, for example — we promote worthwhile goals while promoting ourselves. But we're not the only ones who can do it effectively. God help us when the American Kennel Club realizes what we've been up to. Can you see it now? *Kill a poodle, go to jail.*

False Imprisonment

George ("Machine Gun") Kelly with escorts, October 1933

You might have been as pissed off as I was that morning had you been pulled over by the stupidest cop in central Florida. Forget that it was barely seven in the morning, and a Sunday morning at that. Forget that there weren't nine vehicles in motion within a radius of five miles of the scene of the crime. If you're the dumbest deputy in Bradford County and you see a bike cross U.S. 301 against a red light, you run his ass down and reach for the ticket book.

I got that, but I'm prepared. You should be too. So when those red lights start flashing, get ready for the next phase. Here are the basic rules: 1) Within five milliseconds of your coming to a halt, take off your helmet to suggest that you're a human being; 2) Don't even *think* about getting off the bike; 3) Have your license, registration, and insurance docs ready before they're requested; and 4) Admit nothing, unless you're experienced in these matters, which you're not.

"You ran a red light back there at 301," he stated. Sometimes they ask you if you know why they yanked you over, hoping to lure you into a confession. This clown didn't rise to even that skill level.

"I did nothing of the sort. The roadbed sensor didn't recognize the presence of my bike. It is therefore defective as a matter of law. In such a case I am required to stop, look both ways, and proceed with caution. That I did. You saw that. And yet you have stopped me nonetheless. With all due respect, you're the one who has some explaining to do."

Tossing the grenade back into the highway patrol's lap rarely does any good, nor did it help in this case. It took the man who protects and serves more than 13 minutes to write the ticket. In all that time not a single car had come through the intersection in my direction. I pointed this out to my detainer when he handed me the ticket. He was unimpressed.

"You have to wait for a car if it won't trip," he said.

"And if it's three in the morning in sleeting rain and I've been sitting there for five hours without a car coming along behind me, I wait?"

"Yes."

"And if my car won't flip it, do I have to wait for a truck or an aircraft carrier?"

"You're not in a car, so I'm not going to worry about that."

"No," I said. "It would seem that common sense is the last thing you worry about. See you on the due date. Don't be late."

Ordinarily when you get to traffic court, it's your word against the guy with the badge. He says you were speeding. You disagree. The judge isn't Solomon. He wasn't there. It's supposed to be equal justice, but it's anything but that. Invariably the judge smacks the defendant under the theory that the cop has no reason to lie, but the accused, an irremediable sociopath, does. That isn't so. It never has been. But it doesn't matter. That's the way the world works. Deal with it.

With an imbedded roadway-sensor ticket, however, you can prove beyond any reasonable doubt that the alleged violation is total and unreconstructed bullshit. You'll have an even better defense if you live in Florida, as I do, but buy me a beer one night at the bar and I'll run that one by you. For now, let's get ready to teach that ignorant cop what the law is.

First, stop feeling guilty. You've got a valid motorcycle operator's permit, a legally registered and licensed bike, full insurance, and an 8th-place finish in the Paris-Dakar rally. You know what you're doing, which is more than the bozo with the siren behind you can say.

Second, you come to a light that is controlled by a buried sensor. They are of two principal types: dipole (two parallel strips) or quadrupole (three — I know "quad" is the Latin prefix for "four," but apparently highway departments don't — strips). If it's a dipole, you aim to run right on top of either the right or left stripe. With a quadrupole, go right down the center. If the light changes, go on your way and stop reading this article.

Third, when the light refuses to turn green, you have a decision to make. Either treat yourself as a victim of a cruel and unfeeling world, as suggested by modern socioeconometric theory, and sit at that light until hell freezes over, or stop, look both ways, and proceed with caution to run right through the dysfunctional son-of-a-bitch with a happy smile on your face. You and your bike are legal; it is not. It is falsely imprisoning you within the meaning of the law. You treat it therefore not as an operating traffic signal but as a stop sign and proceed accordingly.

Fourth, immediately after receiving the citation, call the appropriate substation of the state Department of Transportation and demand that they inspect the control box at the suspect intersection to determine if the sensor is properly calibrated. Get the name, telephone number, and address of the employee who will be responsible for this investigation. If you remember nothing else here, at least remember this: *It does not matter what they discover.* If it is miscalibrated, you win outright. Subpoena the dude who did the work, get an affidavit, or at least have him write a letter to you on DOT stationery. Even if they say nothing is wrong, you still win because it didn't sense the presence of your bike, which leads us to the final step.

Fifth, go back to the intersection with your bike, a video camera, and a tripod. Pick a time of the day or night when the traffic is light, set up the camera, and proceed to run up and down and across and back and forth around and over and through that sensor while the film records no traffic light response whatsoever. I was able to make this recording in broad daylight. For three minutes and 21 seconds — the memory capacity of the digital card — I did loops and figure eights all over the length and width of that miserable quadrupole. In the distant background the red light controlling my lane never twitched. Do you have any idea what an eternity 201 seconds is? Download that video file onto a CD and take it to court with a laptop computer. It will be Exhibit #1. You won't need Exhibit #2 or anything else.

On the morning of my court date I sat on a bench in the hall. Eventually the magistrate's clerk called me into the hearing room. I sat down and began to open a battered leather briefcase that had seen hard duty for more than 20 years in the local and federal courts of the District of Columbia.

"That won't be necessary," the magistrate said. "The officer who wrote this ticket will not be appearing today. The case is dismissed."

I slowly shook my head. "Defendants may not say this to you often," I said, "but I'm really sorry to hear that. I was hoping that you and I could teach this guy something about traffic control devices and Florida law. Now I'll have to content myself with writing a scathing letter to the sheriff. You think that will do any good?"

He smiled. "This was important to you, I take it?"

I told him it was a motorcycle issue. There was no need to waste his time on it. But he said he rode a bike. That was all I needed to hear. My case was decided after all. I won. And so will you.

The Chariot

PHOTO CREDIT: THE AUTHOR

Irv Warden buying his last new bike

It's always the same story: It takes about two-fifths of a second from the moment you realize you're no longer in control of your motorcycle to the moment you're no longer in control of your bowels. This is the ultimate argument against the hotshoe who says he's more competent than anti-lock brake systems. Given all the time in the world, beating ABS isn't that hard. But there's never enough time when the wheels come off.

And, when the clock started counting down for Irv Warden last weekend, his wheel literally *was* coming off. The rear end twitched. Then he was on the ground.

"How long did it take from the pucker to the pavement?" I asked.

"About two-fifths of a second," he said.

Like I said: the same old story.

The accident could hardly have come at a worse time or place. He was riding on I-495, the infamous Washington Beltway, a loop of about 75 miles that stands with the Cross-Bronx Expressway and Los Angeles' I-405 as America's trifecta of hideous highways. Traffic was heavy — rarely is it otherwise — on a Saturday morning, and flowing at 70 mph. Then Irv's world changed.

The R1100S first shuddered, then collapsed in a scream of tearing metal. The bike had been heading to Maryland when the rear wheel decided to go to West Virginia. Irv, the wheel, and what remained of the motorcycle went their separate ways.

One of his toes was smacked by the shifter as he and machine parted company. That's the fortunate part. With my last wreck in 1997 the rear brake lever pinned the inside of my calf, dragged me down the road with the bike, and dug a hole in my leg the size of a hand grenade.

Irv was luckier than I had been, unless you think that sliding down an interstate highway on your back in the middle of traffic doesn't amount to much luck at all. But it was. He hadn't high-sided, he wasn't tumbling ass over elbows; he was wearing the right clothes and equipment (even a Rukka back protector); and following traffic wasn't running over him. Those are silver linings in a dark, leaden cloud.

Having stared death in the face, he walked away. His riding suit was scuffed up but largely intact. The coat beneath it was untouched. Twice in recent years he had tripped on sidewalks and sustained more severe injuries. But it was enough.

"It took me as much as three minutes to decide that I am going to get out of the motorcycle world," he said.

Seven years ago I wrote a column about why people ride bikes. They do, I argued, because their genes are biological black holes. Normal people don't ride motorcycles. If you're on one, there's something wrong with you by definition. I have never met a single rider who wasn't covered with Freudian fingerprints.

Then I considered the simple truth that sooner or later everyone stops riding. Why? Does the psychiatrist gesture hypnotically and cure you? Are those genes improving with age? Of course not. You stop because you run out of your allotment of Bad Days. You're born with a certain number of them. When they're gone, so are you — to the morgue, to the emergency room, or, in Irv's case, to somewhere else.

"I had forgotten about your 'bad days' calculation," he said, "but that is exactly how my thought processes ran."

For a few days I tried to talk him out of a precipitous decision. *You're still in shock. This wasn't your fault. How can you just walk out on what has been a significant physical, emotional, and social part of your life?*

He wasn't impressed. He had dodged a bullet the size of a bowling ball. Time won't be erasing that memory anytime soon.

Still, it's the singer that's off-key, not the song. The baby and the bathwater, remember?

"You need two things to survive as a motorcyclist," he reminded me. "Skill and luck. My skills have always been marginal and I have used up all my luck. Do the math: 0 + 0 = me as a hood ornament on an SUV."

But a ripping tailwind on a fall afternoon, the smell of cut grass, the sun setting behind a mountain, They're not the same things in a car.

"Motorcycling is an activity that I don't enjoy as much as I used to," he replied. "And all the evidence indicates that it is probably going to kill me. It is that simple."

At least Irv had a chance to think about the options calmly and objectively. Motorcycles have put a dozen people I've known in graves in as many years, usually in two-fifths of a second. They had no options whatsoever.

In such cases, when the news circulates on the internet, there is a race to be the first to say, "At least he died doing what he loved." Really? If you knew that your bike would kill you on the way to Wal-Mart this afternoon, wouldn't you think about taking a taxi? Not many things are worth dying for. No motorcycle, not even a BMW, is on that exceedingly short list. Irv knows that.

So I don't blame him. I'm not losing a friend. We'll still do Chinese dinners, he'll paw at his beef with snow peas, and I'll reach for another Mai Tai while pondering the random perversity of the universe.

Besides, I'm not much of a riding companion to anyone these days, as slowly as I clunk down back roads with my own marginal skills and diminishing bag of blind luck. Every day that I am still happy to see the bike is about as much as I can hope for. One day, unless something else nails me first, I'll suddenly realize that I can't go near it any longer. I'll hate the sight of it, fear it, and sell it before the sun goes down. On that last day my store of Bad Days will be in bankruptcy. On that last day we all raise the white flag.

It comes down to this: I'd rather have Irv here in some form than not here in any form. We'll all be not here quickly enough. I recall Andrew Marvell's haunting words from almost 400 years ago:

> But at my back I always hear
> Time's wingèd chariot hurrying near.

It's the distant bell, the faint knock on the door. *Who's there? You? So soon?*

PRIVATE E-LIST – JUNE-JULY 1996

A Summer Ride

Life magazine's concept of a lonely road

I did U.S. 36 today, from Indianapolis to St. Joseph, Missouri, at 4,000 rpm. Ten hours, 500 miles. No muss, no fuss. This is flat land, though now and then a 150-foot hill will appear out of nowhere. The road is needle-straight for miles on end. You can see a bear charge from a thousand yards, but there's nothing you can do about it.

At the hopelessly touristy Hannibal I stopped for a chocolate éclair and settled for a doughnut at a gas station. The generic man came over and said, "I didn't know BMW made motorcycles." I live for this sort of encounter. There might as well be a script.

It's always a man who comments, never a woman, and he's almost always a gentleman of a certain age. Whatever I'm doing, I stop and fix the questioner with my look of extreme Bill Clinton pre-sentencing sincerity.

"BMW not only makes motorcycles," I say, "but they've been making them longer than they've been making cars."

"No kidding," he will say.

"Yes," I say. "Since 1923. It was an airplane engine originally. That's what the logo is, a propeller. But the punitive Treaty of Versailles prevented the Germans from producing military equipment. So they stuck the airplane engine into a bicycle frame, did a few mods, and came up with a design that has survived intact in principle to this very day."

"You don't say!"

"I do say," I say. "Baron von Richthofen had the distinctly recognizable ancestor of this twin-cylinder block in his plane." I don't know that this is true, but it could be and I hope it is and it's a wonderful story irrespective of the truth. The Red Baron, thanks to Snoopy, has name recognition at the Santa Claus level.

"I'll be damned," he will say.

"Five kills qualifies a pilot as an ace. The baron knocked more than 80 men out of the sky. Not even Babe Ruth or Secretariat dominated their competition the way von Richthofen did. If an Allied pilot saw that red triplane in the clouds above him, he was a dead man."

"Wow!" he will say.

"And that engine did it," I say quietly, pointing an accusing finger at the guilty R80G/S block. If a motor could try to repent, mine would be doing it in the Amoco parking lot.

This is a five-minute seminar. No matter how late I'm running, I will always have time for the proselytizing. It's my duty and I fulfill it with happiness. For miles down the road I can see the look on the student's face. BMW has become for him that day more than just a yuppie car. It has become a piece of memorable history.

The effect of gaining 10 feet in altitude with the crossing of every hill in Kansas is that by the time you reach the Colorado border you have risen from sea level at St. Joseph to over 4,000 feet. It is imperceptible. Kansas is nothing but an enormous pool table that falls ever so slightly to the east. All of the states in the plains do the same thing. One day you feel fine; the next day your ears are bleeding.

High on the list of things I didn't expect on this ride was to come into Vernal, Utah, at 3:45 p.m. during the last week of June sopping wet and glaring at a bank thermometer that read 59 degrees. Vernal specializes in dinosaurs and hot dust in the summer, not cold, driving rain.

I'd picked up Mike Kneebone and Tim Moffitt in Denver. They were heading to Salt Lake City to help the organizers run the Utah 1088 endurance rally. We pulled into a gas station. I

raised my dripping visor and said to Mike, "Go to Salt Lake, if you will. For myself, I shall pass no more beyond this point today forever."

"Let's stop for dinner and talk about it," he said. Mike and Tim are trenchermen. For them dinner begins to loom when the waitress takes away the breakfast plates.

They went into the restaurant. I called a motel we'd passed a few blocks earlier and made a reservation for a single. I could see the handwriting on the wall.

My karma was fraying at the edges before my feet hit the ground at 6:30 the next morning. Ugly clouds covered the dawn sky, blackest in the Rockies to the west. The drizzle started at the 11,000-foot Eisenhower Tunnel but backed off quickly. By Glenwood Springs, Colorado, rain to the west became a certainty. We'd been running with a fierce tailwind. Now it turned on a dime and let loose in our teeth. Oddly, it was brief, a mere bucket or two. Turning north out of Rifle,

Mike took the lead from me and began to stretch out. This is the part I hate: Wet, curvy, beaten-to-crap state roads in open range, and Kneebone wants to pick up some time.

Mike and I have ridden the equivalent of 1.5 times around the Earth at the equator together. Our roles are as immutable as the stars. He is the psychiatrist; I am the neurotic patient, gnawing on the edges of the map. As Mike begins to disappear, I will slow down, sulk, and pout. If Mike doesn't want to be caught, he won't be, so I don't try. After a while, he will pull up and wait for me.

I roll up beside him. "You know I just hate it when you ride 88 mph on these wet, stinking roads," I say. Tim stares at me. He knows that Mike has been doing no more than 70. After a few thousand miles with us, Tim knows what's happening. He doesn't say a word.

"You lead," Mike says. So I go 68. Variants of this game have been played for countless miles in the last seven years. In all that time dealing with my childish pranks, I can recall him becoming angry only once. The following day I had a bad crash. I'm sure I was trying to make him feel sorry for me, but he's the psychiatrist and he counseled me only to stop bleeding on his shoe.

Mike decided that he really had to make Salt Lake. When presented a choice, Tim always opts for the one that will hurt. He decided to go with Mike. We made plans to meet for breakfast tomorrow in Heber City.

I rode back to the motel. At a traffic light I could hear the bike blubbing. It's a sign of richness in the carburetion. Too many gasoline molecules are trying to mix with too few air molecules in this thin, high-desert air. It's not as serious as the opposite condition, leanness. With a rich mixture you get black, fouled spark plugs and carbon building up on the pistons. So change the plugs and bead-blast the pistons every 100,000 miles or so. Run too lean, though, and your engine goes non-linear and starts heaving connecting rods into your neighbor's yard.

The rodent Robert Pirsig discussed this in his book, "Sophomoric Zen and the Art of Really Bad Motorcycle Maintenance." He sat on a curb and wondered why his clean plugs in Chicago were so crummy looking in Miles City, Montana. It took a couple of pages before he realized he'd gained a mile in altitude. A few pages later he decided that the proper solution was to change the carb jets, reducing the gasoline flow with smaller diameter screws.

It wasn't the proper solution — dropping the jet needle is usually simpler and cheaper — but that might not have occurred to the rodent Pirsig because he was too busy taking gratuitous potshots at his riding companion, a fellow (almost certainly on a BMW) who preferred to let actual mechanics instead of morons like Pirsig work on his bike. Aside from the general bad taste of Pirsig's comments about his buddy, the jibes violated the Fourth Commandment of Motorcycling: Thou shalt not badmouth thy buddy's bike, nor thy buddy's toolkit, nor his wife, nor his brand of beer, nor his ass, nor anything that is thy buddy's. And for these 300 pages of self-absorbed, whining, error-riddled pap, the rodent Pirsig winds up with a Swiss bank account and an inexhaustible supply of college freshmen waiting to touch the bunioned toes of the master.

I think I'll get up 20 minutes early tomorrow and drop my jet needles. If I'm lucky, maybe someone will pay me three million bucks for my trouble.

Nevada is America's answer to Australia, a wild, bawdy place where everything is for sale including, legally, things that are mentioned only as footnotes in the Kama Sutra. There are slot machines in church vestibules. I like that in a church. It tends to blur the distinction, never clear to begin with, between the hereafter and the now-or-never.

Everyone likes Nevada. Half of California rolls in to Las Vegas or Reno on the weekends to throw money at dreams. The military seems to own half the territory and bombs its real estate to bits with boyish glee. Motorcyclists flock here

Jan Cutler at the start of the Nevada 1100, May 1989

for Jan Cutler's insane rallies. Oddly, in this most libertarian of states, bikers are required to wear helmets. Of all the things not to worry about in Carson City, I would think a squashed rider on one of these deserted roads would be at the bottom of the list. The poor guy might not be found for weeks.

I had awakened intending to ride to Arizona but in a period of half a second at an exit ramp on I-15, I decided to ride to Nevada instead. This is how I plan a good trip; a rotten ride is ordained to the millimeter and microsecond months in advance and never involves a near-miss at an off-ramp.

I rode a small, lonely road south to Delta. It is a town on the edge of absolutely nothing. From there the conjoined U.S. 6 and U.S. 50 highways run west into The Void. Look at a map. If you can find a more isolated area in the contiguous United States, please tell me. I love this road like a brother.

Eight miles west of Delta is the last tree. You won't find another until the west side of Sacramento Pass in Nevada, 100 miles to the west. It is a spectacularly empty land, with a highway as straight as a string running through a moonscape. Ever so slowly you ease toward the first range of mountains, the western border of the Salt Lake Valley. Cresting that reveals a view of an enormous valley between the next mountain range to the west. It is the Great Basin, a national park, though I cannot distinguish it from a hundred other valleys of similar configuration in the southwest. Midway through the basin you cross into Nevada and begin the slow climb to Sacramento Pass. Another valley appears, with Connor's Pass on the far side. Here I always stop.

A magical land lies in front of me. I can't describe it, but I have ridden it in weather so cold that ice crystals were suspended in the air and in summers so hot that I knew my brain would explode. I have been through here at night and at dusk and at dawn. There is no "best" time; if I'm here, it is the best time. I don't know what the magic is. I hope I never learn.

Beyond Connor's the highway slowly climbs again toward Ely at 6,500 feet. There U.S. 6 splits to the south and U.S. 50 continues to the west, across countless ranges of the blindingly beautiful Toiyabe National Forest, through Reno, through the Sierra Nevada, and to Sacramento. There it stops, having begun its journey at the Atlantic Ocean Boardwalk in Ocean City, Maryland. For me the Delta-Reno section of U.S. 50 takes a back seat, and just barely, only to the Cisco-Moab-Blanding-Torrey-Escalante-Panguitch-Hurricane roads in Utah.

But merely writing that reminds me of the pointlessness of sorting out degrees of splendor. Pick a Rembrandt, pick a Vermeer. One is better? Really? I am at the center of roads that I live for. Of my 10 favorite highways in North America, nine of them are within a day's ride of Ely. That might explain why I am here tonight instead of at the North Rim.

On the western outskirts of Ely, Nevada, a road marker says, "U.S. 50 — The Loneliest Road in America." The sobriquet comes from a *Life* magazine story of some years ago. The lust for fame in the human breast is such that any mention by national media, even a sarcastic or defamatory comment, is taken as a badge of pride. The truth is that in Nevada alone there are a dozen or more far lonelier roads than U.S. 50, but that has long ceased to matter. If the *New York Times* proclaimed Newark, New Jersey, to be the festering sewer of North America, it would take only a few days for the city fathers to erect a historical marker to memorialize the remark, and then just a few days after that for the sign to be stolen.

But the sensory deprivation on U.S. 50 is extreme. Nothing abounds but knee-high mesquite, sagebrush, and dirt. Only the topography changes. The highway runs through valleys and north-south mountain ranges without number. They are all the indistinguishable same. I imagine myself to be a microbe maneuvering across a boundless piece of corduroy.

In a note I received from Dean Klein this morning, he recalled that this is why he loves Antarctica: The sameness is so profound that he often cannot tell where his being stops and the landscape begins. That's well put. It describes much of the high desert, a land of existential nothingness that seductively overwhelms the traveler. The entirety of the Australian bush is like this, except that its immensity is almost incomprehensible, an area 75 percent of the size of the United States. It may not be Everyman's idea of paradise, but it's mine.

In Bishop, California, I picked up U.S. 395 south. This road runs south-southwest in a narrow valley bordered by old, bald hills to the east and the impenetrable wall of the Sierra Nevada mountains to the west. If you do not cross these mountains at Lee Vining, your next chance to do so is 200 miles to the south. It is movie-making country. If you need mountains and deserts, perpetual sunshine, radioactive spiders, and 100-foot worms that burrow through the ground at 30 mph, Inyo County is the place to be. Here barely 100 miles separate both the highest and lowest spots in the continental U.S.

The only stain in this majestic land is Manzanar. It is just north of Lone Pine. The historical marker refers to it as a "relocation camp." That is euphemistic government bullshit for "concentration camp." For four years 10,000 people were imprisoned here. Their crime was that they were of Japanese ancestry, though the overwhelming number of prisoners were American citizens. Nine similar camps in the west held an additional 100,000 people. I am aware of no greater desecration of civil rights, perpetuated under color of law in this

Historic entrance to the Manzanar concentration camp

century by the United States government, than this hideous example of insane fear run amok.

The conductor of this horror show, a lawyer of course, was Earl Warren, the attorney-general of California. Under his guidance the homes and personal property of the detainees — not one of whom had ever been convicted of any crime — were forfeit and sold. The state reaped billions from the mass theft. In gratitude California voters made him governor. As a public school student in San Francisco in the 1940s, I said prayers for his good health, immediately after reciting the Pledge of Allegiance. I was praying for Earl Warren, the patron saint of racist apparatchiks.

For actions not nearly so grotesque as Warren's, Nazi Albert Speer took 20 years in the chops at Nuremberg. Warren became chief justice of the Supreme Court. Guilt obviously overcame him. He decided to find meanings in the Constitution that had escaped the understanding of those who had sat in the court during the previous 150 years. He became the left-wing poster boy, headed a presidential assassination commission that stumbled on the right answer for the wrong reasons, and then died. I hope Japanese beetles are eating his face off as he rots in his monstrous grave.

Mike Kneebone says I don't like the curly roads because I have to work too hard. He says that I like the needle highways because they let me think. I think he thinks I think too much. I think he may be right. What I ought to do is stay away from Manzanar and its tear-stained earth and endless wind and tortured memories. But I can't. I lived in Japan for a while. I don't say "Jap" bikes. And I don't pray for Earl Warren's health any longer.

I don't want to go across Imogene Pass on the bike. Mike Kneebone and Greg Frazier do things like that. My idea of stretching an R80G/S to the max is riding across 20 yards of gravel to look at a historical marker that by just reading it will guarantee I'll be pissed off or exhilarated for the next 250 miles.

What can I say? I yam what I yam.

Leaving San Diego I'd originally planned to do the Joshua Tree/Twentynine Palms/Amboy route — an area so desolate that, truly, the California Highway Patrol doesn't even go there — but I have already broken down in that stark desert and was hoping to find someplace that might scare even more shit out of me. So I went to east to Desert Center on I-10. The temperature had gone up to 101. I stuck a trivial amount of gas in the tank, bought another Gatorade — I don't even think about the esteemed Dr Pepper on days like this — and turned north to Needles.

It is hell on Earth here. I was carrying a two-liter Pepsi bottle of water, two half-liter Gatorade bottles, and a big prayer. The clouds were long gone and the heat of midday was fiery. The road temperature had to be 150 degrees or more. And I had a tailwind. Good, you say? Not good. Any wind but a tailwind will dissipate the engine heat. With a tailwind the heat collects and tries to climb up under your visor. The Darien jacket's vents were zippered to the top to contain the moisture of the T-shirt. It's an evaporative sump system that, irrespective of the ambient heat, is good for at least 90 minutes. But the bad signs were there.

By the time I made Needles it was 110 and my resting pulse was 112. This was nearing the dangerous zone. I can't do anything about the ambient air, but my internal temperature is partially controllable. The problem at Needles was that my body temperature was slipping out of my control, and quickly.

I redoused the shirt. U.S. 95 would dump me into Las Vegas, 120 miles due north. I called the Motel 6 on Tropicana and made a reservation. And then I made my first real mistake of the day. I took the business route to Bullhead City instead of the parallel route to the west. It is the kind of mistake that is made when the thought processes are not processing clearly. After nearly 30 miles of blue-hairs in Volvos, 40 mph speed limits, and increasing heat, I pulled over to the side of the road.

A cigarette was unthinkable. In the words of people who know real heat, I was taking "mouse breaths," little things that would minimize searing the lungs. My throat was constricted; A frontal-lobe headache had begun, pulsing with every speeding heartbeat.

My sump system requires that I make a decent speed, particularly since I'm zippered to the gills. I wasn't making it. The solution to all my cares finally appeared when I crossed into Nevada and recovered the real U.S. 95. Almost immediately the road stormed into barren, arid hills, but at least it was altitude. Every 1,000 foot gain normally represents about a two-degree drop in air temperature. I took every foot I could find.

The last miles into Las Vegas — Boulder City and Henderson — were bad, but not as bad as it could have been. I-515 now cuts out the horrible array of traffic lights without end. When the motel came into view, I felt delivered.

Sure, it's a gaudy, horrid, plastic town, Las Vegas is. It throws L.A.-sized traffic at you, all the worse for the searing heat off the asphalt. Kitsch galore, garish triumphant, all constructed on the shifting sands of utterly false hope. But it has lights, the likes of which cannot even be imagined. It changes every day, bigger and grander and more spectacular than the day before. I have watched it evolve for almost 50 years and I never tire of its infinite audacity. If you want to find an oasis that can take some of the sting out of a hard desert day, there are worse places to be than The Strip.

I made the 116 miles from Las Vegas to St. George, Utah, in 90 minutes. I felt good. The bike was muttering. One of these days I'm going to come through here at night. I bet the place has a subtle glow from the above-ground nuclear firecrackers that were triggered over the years in Nevada. The prevailing winds doused southwest Utah with dust from two-thirds of the atoms in the periodic table of the elements, including some that the physicists didn't even know existed. The feds didn't tell anyone what was really happening, apparently under the theory that if you can't say something nice, don't say anything at all. I ate part of a seven-legged cow at a fast-food joint and continued to Cedar City at an unseemly speed.

I'm not going to try to describe what happened next. It would take a pre-Raphaelite poet to do that. One day, when you've been very, very good, take a ride beginning Grand Junction, Colorado, and running into Utah through Cisco, Moab,

Blanding, Hanksville, Torrey, Escalante, and Hurricane. When you reach Hurricane, you can tell your friends that you have just ridden the most spectacularly beautiful set of roads in North America. You can't spit without defacing a national park or monument. Your mouth will be dry because it is hanging open from the unspeakable grandeur through which you pass, mile after unbelievably gorgeous mile. There may be somewhere on Earth that could equal southern Utah, but I doubt it. I know nothing can beat it.

Unfortunately, I had to take the route in reverse and cut out some of the highlights as a concession to the holiday and the shortness of human life. Still, my heart was light for the last 350 miles of the day and I didn't ride so much as float. Ten miles east of Escalante I stopped at The Turnout. It is a 180-degree vista of stunning beauty. You can see 60 miles. I sat down in the dirt and for 10 minutes simply stared at the horizon.

This is what it is all about, the scooter-trash life. This is the moment of purest tranquility, the eye of all the meta-hurricanes that have knocked me flatter than day-old beer for 415,000 miles. It doesn't matter what happened yesterday or what wretchedness lies in wait tomorrow. I rode hard to sit in this dirt. Harder miles are ahead because my butt hurts and I'm sick of Gatorade. There is rain, maybe hail, in the northeast. Maybe it will bite me. Maybe not.

I don't care. I want to sit in this dirt until I commit this scene to perfect, ineradicable, read-only memory. A camera won't help. No lens can take this in. I stare, but as soon as I glance away a new scene overwrites the old.

There's only one thing to do. I have to come back.

A grumpy day dawned with ominous chords coming from the shower in the room next door. Rotten, blue-gray clouds were everywhere. I'd overslept, mispacked, and was doing my best to screw up a day that wasn't 10 minutes old.

As I turned east out of Lawrence, Kansas, the bad mood

took a physical form and clipped the edge of my windscreen. It was a dove. For a few miles I tried to convince myself it had been a stinking pigeon, but I knew. A split second earlier I had narrowly missed its mate. Now there was a dead bird on U.S. 24 and another bird flying around, wondering why its own life had changed so dramatically.

They mate for life, I think.

On the small roads south of I-70 I couldn't get the bird out of my mind. Even the peculiar names of towns like . . . well, Peculiar, didn't cheer me up. Nor did Tightwad, nor Racket, nor Climax Springs ("We Pull Together to Help"), nor Hurricane Deck.

The clouds never broke, nor did the memory of the bird. In southern Missouri I was on the prettiest roads in the Midwest and I felt awful. I can't stand hitting an animal with the bike. It unhinges me. I stop to pick up turtles and carry them to the side of the road where their weird little faces were pointing. Once I even tried to move a tarantula off the road, but a truck hit it before I could turn around.

When people who ride motorcycles speak to those who do not, the image they attempt to convey is that of a freedom-starved rebel seeking to be unleashed from earthly bonds. The biker thinks of wind and stars and the smell of hot rain on a macadam road; the listener thinks of intensive care units and interminable months of rehabilitation. Without ever having ridden a motorcycle, the listener understands intuitively that the natural resting place of a motorcycle is on its side and that of a motorcyclist is in the Trendelenburg position in a neurosurgical ward.

The listener is right. In a microsecond a bird goes down through the operation of luckless chance. A moment later I can be whacked because my number is the next to be called after the dove's. There's no malice in it. It's just the way things are. Millions of dollars changed hands when potential buyers began to believe that you meet the nicest people on a Honda. You can meet a lot of nice people in an emergency room, too.

Even the best riders wind up there. Some of them, like world-champion racer Wayne Rainey, come out in battery-powered wheelchairs.

A hurricane is bearing down on Florida. Its true destination is Morganton, North Carolina, the site of the BMW MOA National Rally that begins in a couple of days. I won't be there. I'm going home to feed Bud, my cat. She has lived for almost 16 years in a cul-de-sac where the chance of being hit by a car is minimal. Two doves live in my back yard. Bud would happily have killed both of them in her prime, but she's slowing down some. We all do.

This long ride ended metaphysically, if not physically, at 12:45 p.m. today when I visited my psychiatrist. His office overlooks the Mississippi River in Chester, Illinois. He's everything you'd want in a shrink: dependable, strong, non-judgmental, and dirt cheap. He is also of the non-directive school. That means he doesn't talk much.

He looks perpetually upriver, as if the slow waters of the Big Muddy hold the answers to riddles that elude even him. He smokes a pipe. A cap perches jauntily on his head. His massive forearms seem ready for any task, the more formidable the better. I have not seen him since the eve of the motorcycle rally in DuQuoin in 1992 when my political enemies had me cornered and my troubles were many. In the ensuing years he seems not to have changed much, except for the accumulation of pigeon shit on his face.

The statue of Popeye is in tribute to his creator, Elzie Segar, a resident of Chester. Popeye was born in the Thimble Theatre in 1929 and will live until evil is eradicated from the Earth. Since that will probably not happen anytime soon, it is all the better for me. I like continuity in the delivery of medical services.

Until mid-afternoon I wandered through the back roads of southern Illinois mostly by compass headings. My average speed was worse than usual. I finally decided that if I didn't

The author consults with his psychiatrist

want to do a 600-mile day tomorrow, the terminal day, I'd have to crank up. I found I-64, closed my eyes, and aimed east at a nosebleed 65 mph. With luck, I might have a decent dinner before dark, and a side order of spinach.

I don't know how to finish this. Most of the time my stories end when the word processor runs out of ink or there's no more Bud Lite in the motel's bathroom sink. Tonight I have lots of ink and beer, but I don't hear any doors closing. In a good story a door always slams shut at the end with a satisfying *whonk*.

Today it was mostly interstates I slogged down, but then I'd find myself on roads not much bigger than a pig path. Unless I concentrated almost to the point of pain, I couldn't recall how I had come to be where I was. Sometimes I wasn't even sure which state I was in.

Early on I knew that this ride had a different set of fingerprints on it. Normally I have a laser memory of roads. I can recite not only where I was but the time, temperature, and yards to go for a first down. Now, and for the better part of the last couple of weeks, I have been riding in a twilight zone of amnesia, in real danger of becoming a mislaid, minor character in a Joycean soap opera. For an anal-retentive, Type-A control junkie, there might be worse fates, but I can't think of one.

Eventually I wandered into Moorefield, then Wardensville. Years ago my brother and I used to rip through the back roads around here at insane speeds on an annual springtime automobile rally, sliding through dirt corners, screaming at each other over the roar of a holed-out muffler, and struggling to stay on time to the hundredth of a minute. I have never felt more alive.

The rally died some 10 years ago. I bought a K bike and began to crunch out miles almost angrily. Mileage contests, 1,000-mile days, endurance runs, the works. If there was something I could do to punish a motorcycle and myself, I'd do it, all the while thinking of my grandmother's manic-depression. She sent those bipolar genes down the pipe to me, her idea of a mirthful inheritance, I just know. It isn't diagnosed; it doesn't have to be.

Four years ago the yin picked the yang off second base. I stopped working, stopped snapping off miles like BBs, and stopped appearing in traffic court with yet another speeding ticket. Things change, the moon comes and goes, and the yin and yang perpetually chase themselves around the infield. Maybe what hair I have left will soon turn blue, and I could once again own a car, a nice Volvo.

Wait a damned minute. A Volvo? I pulled into the driveway, 7,260 miles after leaving it. A Volvo, my ass. Bud, my cat, was on the front porch, disinterested to see me as usual. I scratched her hard little head and walked into the house.

The front door closed behind me. *Whonk.*

KICKSTART MAGAZINE – APRIL 1996

In Praise of Newness

Odometer on the author's BMW K75

Depending on your line of work, there are different indicators that spring has finally kicked winter's ugly butt out the back door. Astronomers think it's when daylight and nightlight hours are equal; gardeners believe it occurs when the first crocus periscopes its head above ground, scanning for lawnmowers; and cat owners happily await the arrival on the back porch of Fluffy's first documented kill of the season.

Waiting for spring is a rite that transcends animal, mineral, and vegetable boundaries. Poets scribble dizzily, sidewalks become softer, and cherry blossoms pile up in drifts like yesterday's ill remembered snow. It's an important time because unlike 98 percent of the content of the six o'clock news, the advent of spring is a legitimate big deal: It is a new start, and we get precious few of those in life.

Since my line of work is motorcycles — their care, feeding, and occasional riding — the indisputable signal for me of spring's certain onset is the appearance of the first Kawasaki ad on TV. With that, I shut down the tube, lever myself off the couch, and head for the garage. There are two bikes there, the newer one 10 years old (roughly 135 dog years). There is a tiny glow in its headlight. I take that to represent a machine's smile, indicating that it too knows that spring has sprung. In truth it's probably just a voltage leak.

Clearly the best way to start the riding season is aboard a new bike. There's nothing quite like the satisfying hum of pristine valves smacking themselves senseless against hardened steel 80 times a second, and the barely perceptible metallic whine of con rod, wrist pin, crankshaft, and piston parts flaking off and heading for a distant magnetic drain plug.

But the best part of the new bike is the odometer. It reads 000003, though your mileage may vary. Now that is what I call a nice, round number. It bespeaks unqualified youth, the departure of a wad of money, and the raw arrogance of obsolescence. "No matter what you had before," it says, "I am *newer.*"

Thus, in anticipation of the first Kawasaki ad, I too have bought a new bike for 1996. It sits gleaming in a plastic bag on my workbench and reads a snooty 000003.

"What ho!" you ask. "A bike in a bag?" Well, obviously, it's not the *whole* bike; it's the part that makes the bike elementally new and worth owning. It's the odo unit. And tonight I shall don my surgical gown and latex gloves; arrange my scalpels, hemostats, rib retractors, and 13 mm wrench; and proceed to transmute an ancient lump of base metal into gold.

[Note: While you may be enthusiastic about swapping odometers at home, our attorneys advise that Mr. Higdon is a certified master wrench who at all times observes righteous safety procedures and who is never more than a telephone call away from actual experts.]

Once the patient is out of the recovery room, the real fun begins. Now you can take your new scooter out on the road of real life and watch history come alive. The first few hundred miles are likely to be dreary, for the Roman Empire's death throes lasted a depressingly long time. In fact, not until your odometer reaches 800 will there be much to cheer about (unless you think that taking pi to five places, as was first done at about 200 miles, is momentously exciting), for it was at that mileage that Charlemagne grabbed Europe by the throat and commenced what we now recognize as European civilization. Unhappily, that society took a hard hit at around 1,350 miles when its population was reduced one third by fleas and bubonic plague.

Things will liven up a bit at 1,452 miles when da Vinci, the patron saint of motorcycles, was born. Ninety miles later, take a glance at the sun. It has been the center of our galaxy since 1,543, according to Nicholas Copernicus' book of that mile, though debate remains on the issue in parts of northern Florida. Stop for lunch and compare Burger King's architecture with that of the Taj Mahal, which was finished at 1,648 miles.

Mile after mile history unfolds in your wake: the Battle of Waterloo (1,815 miles), Darwin's theory (1,859), and the Wright brothers' flight at 1,903 miles. You'll naturally want to pause on the mile you were born and again at 1,974 miles when the terminally rat-like Nixon became an unindicted co conspirator.

It's OK to say, "Wow!" It really is. I've known for years that the way to teach kids history is to give them a new bike. And if you turn them loose for a week, they'll also pick up invaluable lessons in geography, climatology, mechanical engineering, and emergency-room practice.

In time, with luck, their odos will display 1,996, a fine year, for it signals the birth of this new motorcycle magazine, *Kickstart*, one that justifiably may deserve the overused word "unique." Some serious, red-eyed boys and girls have put a lot of effort into transforming a maze of computerized zeroes and ones into this revolutionary medium. One day I may get serious right along with them.

But first I think I'll take the new bike for a hop. By the time I reach the Blue Ridge Parkway, the odo should be reading about 000079. I know I'll hear uncountable tons of volcanic ash raining down on the streets of Pompeii. What a bright, new day that must have been. Wow.

Leader of the Pack

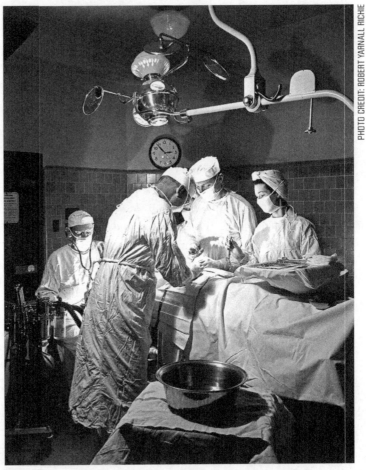

PHOTO CREDIT: ROBERT YARNALL RICHIE

Medical team at work in Brooke Army Hospital, February 1943

In an earlier stage of my metamorphosis, I represented doctors, nurses, and hospitals in lawsuits by disgruntled patients or their survivors. To find out what the medical people were really up to in those Sacred Halls of Heavy Science, I enjoyed spending an occasional Friday or Saturday night looking over their shoulders as they plied their trade.

The weekend, especially in the summer, was prime time for the shock-trauma boys and girls; their clientele would pass the daylight hours getting drunker than a wad of skunks, then do something truly stupid. The resulting injuries were invariably so catastrophic that you could actually plot the decline of the value of Blue Cross stock as the treatment commenced.

Of course, the accident cases I most looked forward to were the motorcycle smashes. They're not common, but when they happen, they're usually unforgettable. I'd show up late in the evening, wearing my helmet, and wait for someone to start in on me. It was like bumping up the voltage on a grid. They'd get excited and start yelling about the machines from Hell and didn't I have the brains God gave a catfish and wasn't I aware that in the health-care industry "motorcyclist" was spelled "organ donor?"

I'd laugh and wait for the ambulance to roll up or the helicopter to land. Sooner or later something would come in. Until then, it was sit and wait and tell morbid jokes with sardonic grins. The usual practice of anesthesiology is 99 percent boredom and 1 percent panic, they say. The ER is sometimes like that. But not often at night.

And not this weekend, at least. The chopper came in just

before midnight and the dance began. He was a biker, too young at 16 to be so unconscious, but still he looked great. An iron-pumper, the beautifully defined muscles around his chest wall said it all. His face was unmarked and perfectly tranquil. I stared at him as the medical bees clumped around in a swarm. He was an Adonis. And they thought he was dying.

To an outsider the scene was pure chaos. But each doctor and nurse had a job, each knew what the drill was, and each understood the edgy bounds of responsibility. To see the whole was to see nothing; to focus on a single segment was to lose the picture. They were trying to keep this kid alive until God could fix him. In the meantime they adhered to Rule No. 1: In a medical emergency the first blood pressure you take is your own.

Marianne, the helicopter nurse, was pulling off her jump suit. She was a witness in a case I was defending. We'd downed a few beers along the way for trial preparation.

"His father told him not to ride," she said. "Locked the bike in the garage. But the kid found the key."

A nurse was running an internal catheter, hoping not to find blood in the bladder. A resident was prepping the stomach for a belly tap. The neurologist was poking, the on-call surgeon was paged, the anesthetist rocked back and forth on his heels, waiting.

"Picked up his girlfriend. Was on the shoulder of U.S. 50 and hit the back of a stalled flat-bed. Went from 40 mph to zero in a tenth of a second."

"The girl?" I asked.

The EKG leads were jellied and placed. Portable X-ray machines emitted a small hissing sound.

"Not a scratch," she said. She looked at me curiously. "When are you going to get rid of that thing?"

"You know me," I said.

Marion Jordan came into the suite, a definite long-ball hitter, director of the hospital's burn unit, and the ringmaster on tonight's shift. He walked over to the table, taking the scene in. A pack of surgical residents gathered around, pretending they weren't gathering around. Jordan was a traumatologist by training. He'd seen it all. He was seeing it again.

At 40 rounds a second a resident rattled off the history, vital signs, and an almanac of symptomatology. Jordan stared at the EKG strip.

"Yeah," he said, making the word into three syllables. He's from Georgia. "The sternum bruised his heart. A good whack." He turned to a resident. "Belly tap?"

"Positive." Internal organs were bleeding into the peritoneal cavity. Not good.

"OK," Jordan said heavily. "Got the head shots?"

A resident scurried away.

Marion looked at me. "Well," he said, "are you ever coming to Daytona with me?" He'd run the first-aid tent at the track during Bike Week for years and had seven dirt bikes in his garage.

"I can't next year," I said. "Judge set a trial. I begged him not to."

"It'll settle," he said.

"Maybe."

The resident returned with the head films. Marion jammed them onto the X-ray view box and flipped on the lights casually. The residents, arcing around him like baby ducks, looked at the shadows.

"See this?" he said, pointing at the kid's jaw. Eight heads nodded. "Fractured mandible." The heads nodded and waited. Marion paused reflectively. "It'll be a while before this boy eats anything but grits."

No one wanted to laugh, but it was impossible not to smile. With just a phrase the tension in the room seemed to lessen. I'd seen it in operating rooms, when the surgeon kicks open the door and enters the ring like a matador. There's nothing like it. Pomp and circumstance, life and death.

"Get him to the OR," Marion ordered. "We'll have him back on his bike in a while. If his father doesn't hang him first."

I looked at Marianne. She was staring at the floor, shaking her head in disbelief.

At 4:00 in the morning, when even the drunks were too blown away to hurt themselves any further, I walked out to the parking lot and started the bike. On the way home I looked for disabled trucks on the shoulder.

[Postscript: Marion's burn unit was the subject of international acclaim for its treatment of survivors of the September 11, 2001, attack on the Pentagon. On September 28, 2018, he was killed following a minor automobile accident on I-97 north of Annapolis, Maryland. He and the other driver had stopped their cars to trade insurance information. They were standing on the shoulder of the highway when they were struck by a following vehicle.]

ON THE LEVEL – APRIL 2003

Your Own Ride

In the organizational meeting that established the BMW Bik-ers of Metropolitan Washington 29 years ago, one of the stated goals was "safe motorcycle riding." Periodically we try to deal with the difficult task of coordinating individual and group styles. Some clubs may have achieved that happy objective; we haven't come close. Like many organizations, ours doesn't have anything resembling a group consciousness. You'd have better luck trying to herd cats.

Still, we try, sort of. Last year a few of us attended a group-riding seminar being run by a local Harley club. Our safety-committee chairman subsequently cranked out a series of columns about the elements of riding in a crowd. For all the interest generated by the topic, he might as well have been writing in Sanskrit.

While there are innumerable rules, tenets, regulations, doctrines, options, tips, codes, by-laws, disciplines, opinions, suggestions, and multi-layered exceptions to all of the forego-ing, the ultimate fallback position in group-riding theory is that every rider is responsible for his own ride. When you chant those magic words, all bets are off. It is too often invoked for one and only one purpose: to excuse the conduct, no matter how negligent or illegal, of the group as a whole and the ride leader in particular. The result is that when the pack heads out, no one but the individual will be to blame for what hap-pens next.

I admire that kind of *reductio ad absurdum* reasoning, don't you? It employs an unassailable principle of law that has been with us since the 14th century, sounding mortally profound while utterly ignoring what happens when a ride morphs from one rider into many. Individual egos immediately take over, and what little is left of the original group dynamic can just go piss up a rope.

Sure, the basic design is good. Every rider is equipped, or at least as equipped as a motorcyclist ever can be. The route is known. Turn-by-turn instruction sheets are issued. There are designated regrouping points. This is a ride in which the principle of individual responsibility has some actual meaning. If you don't like the pressure or if you want more of it, drop out and go your own way. We'll see you later.

But most groups rides aren't like that at all. They are hastily arranged affairs where the law of the jungle applies in full fury. Someone will step forward to lead. It's always a guy whose self-image is that of Alpha Male. In our club it's Racer X, though that is not his real name. He, or a cousin of his, belongs to your club. He says he knows the way from where you are to where you want to be. No one else has a clue. Do you have any doubt how this is going to end? Given the wholesale failure of structure at the outset, no one should be surprised at the resultant chaos. Someone is going to get popped, but good.

The normal peer pressure that bubbles when the group sits on the flight deck becomes a living creature. Adrenal glands begin to glow. It can't be helped. You have no more control over the ensuing hormonal rush than you do over the phases of the moon. If you can't stay glued to the rider ahead of you, you're weak, and soon everybody will know it.

It gets worse. If you lag too far behind, you're going to be lost as well. Anyone who can ride as contemptuously as that guy in the front isn't likely to spend much time at the next intersection worrying about whether you're still in tow. If you do eventually find your way to the finish, the crowd will have a good chuckle as you slink in. The big ego that was your passenger 15 minutes ago is now looking for a place to hide.

And if you're the poor guy who simply *has* to get to the finish for some reason — to see Jimmy's soccer game, to mow a lawn that hasn't been cut in nine weeks, or to be on time for a group therapy session — you will do whatever it takes to maintain the pace. With that decision, your security flag changes from green to red. You will soon discover that it's the tension, not the speed, that will shortly be putting you in the hospital. The speed merely adds to the time it takes before you're discharged.

Speaking for mineownself, I avoid riding with people I don't know, especially guys like Racer X, unless I have no real choice. I don't want them to show me their best stuff and I want even less the incessant pressure of trying to keep up. There are surprises enough in the ordinary trip from A to B to last me a lifetime. Why would I want to add another level of uncertainty to an already insanely dangerous sport?

There's an additional problem. Racer X and I almost certainly don't agree on what our responsibilities are. I, for example, may naively believe that since he has volunteered to lead us to our destination, then he has assumed a duty to do so reasonably and safely. He, contrarily, may think his duty is to do it as fast as he can. He may also think my duty is to keep up, while I view my role as being somewhat less aggressive. I'm hoping that he's thinking about all of the ducks lined up behind him, but my guess is that he's just thinking about how fast he can punch into that next corner. In such cases, when I can't be sure that I'm on the same page as everyone else, I stop reading altogether. I suggest you do the same.

But you didn't listen to me, did you? Now you'll be sucking dinner through a straw in the rehab unit for the next five months. Will you persist in believing that you were responsible for your own ride? You were, in some legal and metaphysical sense, I suppose. Taking a cosmic view, however, the fates had arranged to put you in the worst of all possible positions. You will be paying for it for the rest of your life. And on every one of those long, painful days, a fellow motorcyclist will no doubt be pleased to remind you that it was all your own fault.

There's only one person who can change this sordid mess, and his name is You. Racer X and his ilk aren't about to conform their behavior to the minimum standards of biker, much less social, propriety. They can't. You might as well try to teach an orangutan to sing the Pilgrim's Chorus from *Tannhäuser*. Pretend you're Nancy Reagan: Just say no. It may hurt a little for a while, but it's better than hurting a lot forever.

A Winter Ride

Everything changes.

The weather improved so much yesterday afternoon I began to think I was on a different but related planet. The sun was out today. I didn't recognize it for a while. The wind wasn't dissin' me so much. For about a half-hour it was almost a tailwind.

The bike seemed not to be so angry today. Heat had apparently loosened up some of the steering-head bearing glue. The gas mileage was up on one tank this afternoon by 55 percent over a few days ago.

My mood improved. A lot. My blood pressure, low to begin with (oddly enough), always drops another 20 points when I come into Mississippi. It's the ancient homeland and I like it here. I like the slow roads and the quiet farms and the old pine forests. It relaxes me. It's a pretty place.

For at least 10 generations Higdons have been begetting themselves here. I was the first kid in the paternal line born outside the deepest, darkest south in 270 years, and even then I was still announced below the Mason-Dixon line, though barely.

My grandfather used to deliver babies in the little town of Brookhaven. When the Depression hit, the proud parents would pay the bill with chickens or corn. My father was born here in a house at 306 S. Jackson Street. One of my fraternity brothers at Ole Miss years ago was Robert Higdon Boling. My grandfather delivered his father.

When my father was in the army, having left Brookhaven for the bright lights, we would periodically come back here to visit his uncle, my great-uncle, who lived at 515 S. Jackson Street. Being army people, we had no actual home, so we used that address as our legal residence. I used it when I turned 18 and registered for the draft. I never was called. Years later I realized that my draft board had probably rounded up every black kid in Lincoln county before thinking about calling the white boy whose great-uncle was the president of the Brookhaven Bank & Trust Company and whose daddy had fought in the Battle of the Bulge.

I have left footprints all over this town, visible only in the fourth dimension. One summer when we were here I'd just finished reading *Beau Geste*. By blind luck I discovered that the movie was playing at the Haven. I *had* to see it. But no, said the old man. I'd mouthed off or something and was grounded. It took me about three years to get over that one.

My footprints are hard to find now. Everything has changed. Uncle Charles is in the graveyard and workmen are climbing all over the roof of his house, erecting an ugly garret. A real-estate office is infecting my father's house. The Haven is a beauty salon. The bank was bought by a chain. It says "Trustmark" but it's not a mark I'd trust. I-55 screams by to the west, in an awful hurry to get to New Orleans, and a strip of wall-to-wall franchises leads into the sleepy old Brookhaven downtown area of about four square blocks.

Heraclitus said that you can't step in the same river twice. I keep trying because he was just some old Greek dude and you never know. Tomorrow I'll run down Route 51 to McComb and pass Dixie Springs where I learned how to hate fishing. Dixie Springs will still be there, I bet. And I still hate fishing.

My mood was positively chipper when I rolled out of Del Rio, Texas, this morning. The temperature was in the high 80s, right where God intended. It was nearly perfect, but for a gusty wind that couldn't decide whether to smash my nose or left ear. I didn't much mind. All the other elements were harmonic for a change.

In an hour I came to Langtry and turned into the village to visit Judge Roy Bean's spirit. He was a sociopath hired by the railroads to bring some order to the territory and he did just that. He didn't hang miscreants; he fined them everything they had, including horse and gun, then expelled them from town. In late 19th-century West Texas, that was tantamount to a death sentence. Bean kept the fines.

He was infatuated with the English actress Lillie Langtry. He would get drunk and write her long, lugubrious letters. He named the town for her. Finally, in January 1904, she came to visit, but by then Bean had been dead nearly a year.

On my way out of the visitor's center, I became involved in a little geopolitical theory with a pleasant staffer of a certain age. I asked her why Texans seemed to be so excited about the Alamo when, it seemed to me, all Santa Ana had been trying to do was to expel a bunch of rowdy invaders from his country. She stared at me, horrified at the blasphemy.

"They were fighting for Texas," she finally said.

"Except that Texas then belonged to Mexico, right?"

I was about to advise her of my belief that Stalin had a better right to march into Czechoslovakia in 1948 than did Abe Lincoln when he sent Union troops to Manassas, Virginia. Sanity overcame me fortunately and I rode out of town, having thought enough about Manifest Destiny for one day.

In my next metamorphosis I have decided not to return as a lightning bug as I had originally planned. No. Now I want to return as a national park concessionaire. I don't care which park or what concession. Give me one good season screwing the socks off the traveling public and I can retire in Bimini, drinking Goombay Smashes until my liver looks worse than Mickey Mantle's. These concessionaires have raised the rip-off to an art form. They could teach scams to factory-outlet stores.

The room here at the Chisos Mountain Lodge in Big Bend National Park is nice. It has two large beds, so I'll probably switch from one to the other at three in the morning. I'd reserved a smoking room, hoping that I could get one that was not only smoking but actually afire. They gave me a room that didn't smoke at all. All right. I know how to fix that.

They told me where the ice machine was. They didn't tell me it wasn't working. I would have called room service but I don't have a phone and they don't have room service. So I took my room key and ice bucket and got a load from the restaurant. I returned to the room and learned that my room key was from the Motel 6 in Del Rio. I'd forgotten to turn it in. My real room key was on my beds. Back to the front desk.

I think there's a pretty steamy movie on HBO tonight. I would watch it except this room doesn't have HBO. It doesn't have a TV, either. I can listen to the radio because I carry a King Kong Sony shortwave. I can also add up the day's expenses on the palmtop computer. For the room I will enter $59.36.

What the hell. Big Bend is spectacularly beautiful. It doesn't matter what things cost or how many insignificant irritants I have to stare down. I'm lucky to be here. I'm lucky to have gorgeous places to visit and this is one of the very best. It combines what I like above all in a park: searing loneliness, desert, mountains, brutal heat, clean roads, and 80 different things that can kill you with minimal effort.

Big Bend isn't for everyone. It takes a real commitment to come here, since it is about as far out in the sticks as you can get and still be in the continental U.S. El Paso is the nearest town, if you count that hole as a town instead of a dirt farm with railroad tracks, which it is. No. This place is a long way from nowhere. They have signs telling you how far it is to the next gas station. That is beyond rural in my book.

And once you arrive, the park takes some getting used to. It's ancient. The average rock is 35 trillion years old. Unlike other old rocks, the ones here actually *look* old. They are missing a lot of teeth and they don't seem happy about it. They are rocks with an attitude.

The weather is routinely awful. Wild temperature ranges are common. It swung 55 degrees yesterday. When it rains,

there are flash floods. When it doesn't rain, there are dust storms. It could snow tomorrow or be nine million degrees. Nobody knows. It is the toughest sort of land imaginable. I cannot begin to understand how the first settlers could ever have called this moonscape home.

There are 17 motels in Van Horn, Texas, and 22 restaurants, but most people don't stop except for gas. The length of town is about 1.2 miles and there are no traffic lights. When you walk along the road, people wave at you from their pickups. It is the middle of the great West Texas void. Maybe they're lonely and are trying to make a new friend. I wave back.

For a town this small, you might think that it would be bereft of history. But a lot has happened to me here. In 1950 it was the scene of The Great Swordfish Steak Dinner Disaster that ultimately propelled two members of my family into 12-step programs. In mid-January of 1993 I came out of the icy, fog-shrouded Davis Mountains to the east with a lust for Chuy's gorditas rattling around in my hypothermic brain.

I always stay at the Seven Kay Motel. It's a generic Asian-Indian dump that caters to pre-homeless people, truckers, and bike scum. But I know the phones will work. They have ice, HBO, and the Weather Channel. I have never seen a scorpion in the room, and that's more than I can say for a million-dollar home I stayed in one night in Houston.

The best part of the Seven Kay is that it's across the street from Chuy's, the finest Tex-Mex restaurant anywhere. Normally I don't give a damn about food on the road. I eat like a dog and spend about seven dollars a day on kibble. But if I know I'm heading for Van Horn, I'll starve myself all day. I hide the dry roasted peanuts in a saddlebag and drink less than a quart of Dr Pepper. By the time I hit Chuy's, I could eat the menu.

Jeff Brody, whose opinion in these matters is due some deference, says that Chuy's is not only not the undisputed world champ of Tex-Mex, it is not even the best Tex-Mex in Van Horn. Sportscaster and noted fat guy John Madden disagrees. He has Chuy's listed in his Haul [sic] of Fame. He likes fajitas. Me, I hold with the gorditas. I don't know what they are; I just eat them and write stories about them.

I graduated from Wilson High School in the District of Columbia. We were the Tigers. The tiger is not an inhabitant of D.C. except at the zoo. Why anyone would pick a tiger for a school that has nothing to do with such an animal escapes me. I can understand the Van Horn (Texas) Eagles. There are eagles in West Texas. The school may even have one in a cage. My school did not have even any paper tigers.

My school's mascot was decided before Mayor-for-Life Marion Barry oozed onto the political scene. He would have picked the Crack Whores, Lifers, or Dime Bags as a mascot. In all candor I think those names are more suggestive of the spirit of the community than any tiger ever roaming the streets of D.C.

I see similar oddities when I ride around on the lost roads, the ones that William Least Heat Moon called "blue highways." There were a lot of them in the little towns in Louisiana that I have passed through recently. In Dry Prong they are Wildcats. Jonesville likes Black Bears. Vidalia opts for the alliterative Vikings, a rival of the nearby Ferriday Trojans.

Now think about that for a moment, because I have hundreds of miles each day to do just that and it's about time you see what I have to look forward to when I'm putting my boots on in the morning. When was the last time a Trojan was sighted within 5,000 miles of Ferriday, Louisiana, except at the Rexall drug store? Never, that's when.

But it gets better. The girls' — is it proper to refer to high-school females as "girls," like I care? — basketball team, according to a two-day-old newspaper I was reading this afternoon in the Vidalia McDonald's, was in the state championship finals, and is known as the "Lady Trojans." I don't know about their chances in the game, but their name alone makes them a winner in my book.

Jena has Giants. Across the river it's no different. In Natchez they are Bulldogs. You see them on the water towers or on a sign at the edge of town or on a schedule billboard by the school: Sidewinders, Scorpions, Lions, Indians, Jaguars, Gila Monsters, Pumas, Spiders, Falcons, Terriers, and so on. Are you beginning to see a common theme in these names? The mascots are things that we fear and dread and detest.

Even Belfrey, Montana, a town of about nine people, is not immune. It is the home of — I'm not making this up — the

Bats. Everyone knows that such creatures seek out women's hair, entangle themselves therein until the scalp is ripped asunder, and leave bloody, rabid bites in the skull.

The exceptions appear only to prove the rule. At the University of California (Santa Cruz) they are the Banana Slugs. I've been there and I can tell you that there are more unsolved murders around that campus than anywhere else in the country, even the University (pause for chuckle) of the District of Columbia.

I want to ride through peaceful towns tomorrow. I want to see some high schools that promote the happiness and joy that come from being in America, from being able to remember 50 percent of the words of the Star Spangled Banner even if ordinary citizens can't sing it very well. I want to see mascots that we can all trust and in whom we can find comfort.

So give me not the Beaumont Bandits but the Breasts. No more of the Amarillo Anthrax. They're the Amphetamines now, along with the Birmingham Bud Lites, the Chattanooga Chocolate Chips, Tampa Trailer Trollops, McAllen McNuggets, and Nashville Negative Pap Smears.

The last two days on the road were some of the worst motorcycling I've ever been through. It was cold, windy, and lethally boring. When I rolled into my driveway, I was shivering uncontrollably. There was snow in the yard. I left home in the middle of winter, February 11. I returned with the first day of spring on the horizon. You wouldn't know it. It's colder today than the day I left.

I know, I know. If you don't want to be cold, try riding through Kansas in July, not through Cloudcroft in February. If someone else were telling me this story of woe, I'd have less than a vanishing trace of sympathy. But it did seem that much of this trip had a conspiratorial flavor to it, one designed to drive me nuts. It worked. There isn't a cell in my body that doesn't hurt right now.

Mike Kneebone keeps telling me that it isn't the bike I hate. It's the weather, he says. Maybe. But I can't remember more than one or two good rides that I've had in the last five years. I don't care how you define "good rides." They are escaping me.

Some years ago, at the very pinnacle of his career, Philadelphia Eagles football coach Dick Vermeil walked away and never looked back. He said, in effect, that his yin and yang weren't in balance. Winning and losing were gravely disproportionate. The highs, he said, lasted for a few hours; the lows hung around for weeks. It wasn't worth it.

I've been thinking about Vermeil a lot lately.

The Four Deadly Sins

Bike Week, 1996

[*Author's note: This column is dedicated to the memory of Simon Milward, the most selfless, generous, and cheerfully optimistic man I have ever known. On January 1, 2000, he began what was to have been an 18-month trek around the world on a homemade motorcycle, raising money for poor villages that could not afford even the most rudimentary medical and nursing care. On March 4, 2005, still on the road, still penniless, and still hoping to return to his beloved England by October, he was killed in a traffic accident in the West African country of Mali. Thousands of miles away in a land so foreign as to be utterly incomprehensible to the average citizen of Mali, the sun was rising on the first day of Bike Week.*]

The scorpion is a dangerous, amoral creature whose principal function is to serve as a poison delivery system to anything that crosses its path, not unlike an ex-wife. The animal — an arachnid, not an insect — has a hard, chitinous exoskeleton that makes swimming difficult, thus giving rise to the ancient story of a scorpion waiting by a riverbank, seeking a way to the other side. A frog hops by. The scorpion asks for a lift across the water on the frog's back.

"Not a chance," the frog laughs. "You're a scorpion. You'd spike me before we reach the other side."

"Think it through: If I sting you, we'll both drown."

The frog reluctantly agrees that there is merit in the scorpion's argument. They enter the river. Halfway across, the scorpion spears the frog in the back of the neck.

"You fool, you've killed us both!" the frog says with his dying breath.

"I can't help it," the scorpion replies. "It's what I do."

Beyond the terrible truism that no good deed goes unpunished, the fact remains that consummate evil really does exist. You cannot reason or negotiate with it. Merely being in its presence is a threat to your health and well-being, much like standing between a congressman and a television camera.

But, as I noted at the outset, the scorpion is an amoral, not immoral, being. It acts out of biological imperative, not corrupt motive. Its polar opposite is Popeye, who cannot help but thwart wickedness wherever it may lurk. Unlike the perpetually self-aggrandizing Jimmy Carter, Popeye seeks no earthly acclaim for his efforts. "I yam what I yam," says the mythic sailor. "It's what I do," says the scorpion. They move toward their goals with clinical precision; they are both objects of awe; and yet the results of their labors could not be more different. Popeye gives hope to humanity; the scorpion takes it away.

When evil and corrupt motive combine, there is sin. Pope Gregory the Great analyzed the problem in the sixth century, coming up with a deadly list: anger, sloth, pride, greed, lust, envy, and gluttony. Die with one of those unforgiven and you roast.

Some of these clearly are unique. Anger is like no other sin. It's the same with sloth. Pride stands by itself, as one would expect. But greed, lust, envy, and gluttony seem to me to be variations on an acquisitive theme. So, although I admittedly lack post-doctoral training in theology (or post-graduate training, or undergraduate training, or *any* training, for that matter), I have taken the liberty of revising Pope Gregory's work in the interests of clarity and economy. Henceforth we will have just four deadly sins: anger, sloth, pride, and Bike Week.

It starts on the first Friday of March, sometimes a week earlier. It's easy to tell, even without a calendar. Get gas in Daytona on Thursday night. If the price has gone up 10 cents a gallon by the following morning, it's Bike Week.

Or take a ride up Atlantic Avenue. If the sign that was

advertising a $25 room at the Sand Flea Motel yesterday now says "Great rates!" it's Bike Week. Sure, $125 a night with a four-night minimum might not seem like a great rate to you, but it'll be $150 next year. Don't worry about the blood-stained rug, the shredded curtains, or the broken mirror in the bathroom. Those are free, as are the fleas. Think of them as the motel's mascots.

If you wear earplugs when you drift off to dreamland, you probably won't hear the woman screaming in the parking lot at 4:00 a.m. She'd be

Bike Week, 1996

drowned out anyway by the unmuffled Harleys that roll up and down Atlantic Avenue 23 hours a day, looking for love in all the wrong places.

You'll also know it's Bike Week when the vendor tents at the track spring up like mushrooms after a hard rain. Curiously, it seemed this year as if the crop was perhaps one-third its former size. I asked Adventure Motorcycle Gear's Frank Cooper what had happened.

"They wanted to increase our rent somewhat," he said. "Last year we paid $950 for a 10x10 stall. This year they were demanding $1,450."

For our arithmetically challenged readers, that works out to an inflation rate of 53 percent, marginally worse than the three percent experienced in the rest of the United States. If Alan Greenspan knew what was going on in Daytona during Bike Week, he'd hang himself.

"So where did you go?" I asked.

"Holiday Travel Park," he said.

Ah, yes. That place. It is trying to be the successor to the Bulow campground, sanctified territory, or at least as sanctified as a spot can be that used to host a bunch of motorcyclists in tents. I think it was founded by Ponce de Leon in 1513 — *bullo* being, I think, the Spanish word for "extortion" — but I might be in error. This much is certain: It ultimately became a winter watering hole for the BMW crowd and the home of one of the largest annual Beemer rallies in North America.

The Space Coast club ran things, after a fashion, but it was as tiring and thankless a job as herding cats. It was never about making money; for them it was about controlling losses. But Bulow evolved over the years into a larger-than-life happening. I always thought of it as the equivalent of Rick's Café in Casablanca. If you sat at a table there, sooner or later the entire world would walk by.

The death rattle came in 2000. The Coasties couldn't take it any longer. "Every year that I drove up there with the tent and supplies was the longest day of my life," former BMW RA president Ed Jorgensen says. "I could never get a contract out of them ahead of time. I never knew what would happen. All I could count on was trouble."

That year, on Bike Week's last Saturday morning, Richard Sainct rolled into the campground on the motorcycle he'd used to win the Paris-Dakar rally six weeks earlier. A huge crowd had gathered. Robert Hellman was simultaneously translating French for Sainct, German for some *Motorrad* guy, and English for the rest of us. I stood there and smiled. *I'll never see anything like this again,* I told myself.

And, of course, I haven't. As bad a writer as he was, and he could be positively horrid when his blood-alcohol level reached 0.27 percent, Thomas Wolfe at least got this one right: You really can't go home again. Those days are gone, Jack. And they ain't coming back.

Daytona has been a significant part of my life for these past 15 years. First I came here because I was a biker and bikers came to Daytona for Bike Week. I went to Main Street and

(L-R) Robert Hellman, the author, and Richard Sainct at Bulow campground during Bike Week, 2000. Six weeks earlier Sainct had won his second Paris-Dakar Rally on the BMW F650 in the foreground.

the beach and the track and the American Motorcycle Institute (AMI) and the Cabbage Patch and the campground at Bulow. I came back the next year and did everything all over again. Same for the third year. By the fourth year I was a student at AMI, and in subsequent years I'd come back because I wanted to see my old AMI friends. A couple of years ago I bought a condo in Daytona Beach Shores. Tonight I take a break from the computer, walk out onto the balcony, and stare at the sea. On a very clear day, I'm pretty sure I can just make out the west coast of Africa. Give me a little more elevation and I might be able to see where Simon died.

Still, time has a way of slipping beyond your grasp. Following the death of his wife a few years ago, and shortly after a godsend of a second marriage, Lamar Williams, AMI's owner and a close personal friend of mine, decided to sell the school. The new occupants, corporate suits with an eye to nothing but the bottom line, cancelled the fantastic party that was *the* place to be on Thursday night during Bike Week. They halted the Brute Horsepower Shootout. They shut down the school's shop where you could run into legends like Armen Amirian, Dave Roper, and Nick Ienatsch sweating over a Heli-Coil and trying to wring a few more horses out of an AHRMA bike. Lamar threw money at Bike Week like it was confetti. These new guys? If it's not generating a buck, it's history. Can't help it. It's what we do.

After you've seen a few Japanese bikes run without oil until the engines seize and then dropped 75 feet from a crane onto a manure-soaked field to the cheers of a mob of drunken Harley riders, you may revise that idea of a brotherhood of bikers. You've been to one Bike Week too many if you're watching women wrestle in a pit of cole slaw and you're hoping those bras *won't* come off. Bulow bit the dust, the Visigoths sacked Rick's Café, and the Holiday Travel Park now charges visitors $5 to come in and wander around for four hours, looking for the ghosts of Bike Week past. Not even Bulow ever dreamed up a scam that raw. Next year it'll probably be $10 for two hours. Can't help it. It's what we do.

The last hope I had to reconcile myself to Bike Week was the Iron Butt Association's dinner. In the old days we'd pull a few tables together on Friday night at Stavro's pizza joint at Beach and Orange and a dozen of us would tell lies about rides we'd never taken and places we'd never been. Couldn't help it. It was what we did. In recent years the party had grown to the point where we were renting Elk halls and preparing menus for a sit-down dinner for 300 of our closest friends.

It's my job each year to take the microphone after dinner and introduce the IBA's founder and president, Mike Knee-bone. This year I made some preliminary comments about Bike Week gouging, noise, motel fleas, and easy examinations you can do in the privacy of your own home to recognize the onset of the secondary stage of syphilis.

I then asked for a show of hands. "How many of you would be here tonight if Mike Kneebone had stayed home in Chicago?"

There were about 250 people in the room. They are some of the toughest riders I know. They will ride anywhere, any-time, just for the love of riding. If Daytona loses this kind of motorcyclist, what is Bike Week's real future?

Ten of them raised their hands.

It was dark when I rode back home that night. The sun had long since set on all kinds of things. I knew it would be the last Bike Week I would ever see. There are cancer cells that destroy the host, and in the process destroy themselves. I wondered, *What sort of organism could orchestrate its own extinction?* And, when I rode past the "Vacancy" sign at the Sand Flea Motel and heard the woman screaming in the parking lot, I remembered the fourth deadly sin.

IRON BUTT MAGAZINE – MARCH 2012

This Thing We Do

The Abernathy kids

It seems that when I ride lately I spend a disproportionate amount of time wondering why I ride at all. In all the years I've been searching for what motivates people to climb on motorcycles I've yet to encounter even one explanation that makes a grain of sense. Freedom? Wind in hair? Open road? I'm sorry. Those words might as well be Latvian.

Even more mystifying to me is the cult of the Iron Butt rider, yet it attracts me in a way that no religion ever has. I've spent the last 25 years hanging around such people, studying their behavior, learning their dialect, but I am no closer today to having a clue about the essence of this than I was at the beginning.

I can't even define what "endurance" is, though during my introductory talk at the annual IBA pizza party during Bike Week this year, I gave it a try. I mentioned the exploits of two brothers, Louis and Temple Abernathy, who in 1909 rode from their home in Oklahoma to Santa Fe, New Mexico, and back. It took them more than two months to do the 1,600 miles, foraging for food along the way and camping out most nights. Sure, they were on horses, not motorcycles, but wouldn't you call that an endurance ride? Perhaps I should mention that at the time of their adventure Louis was nine years old and Temple was five. Years later in an interview Temple said, "But I was an *old* five." And, of course, they very quickly became celebrities.

The following year they rode their horses to New York and drove back to Oklahoma in a Brush motor car, two chil-

Blaine Paulus

dren in a chain-driven, one-cylinder vehicle on a 2,000-mile ride at a time in American auto history when highways were frequently not much more than mud tracks. They met mayors and governors and adoring women, surrogate mothers all, but Temple finally drew a line: "No more kissing," he said.

It still wasn't enough for them. The next year they were offered a $10,000 prize if they could ride on horseback from New York to San Francisco in 60 days. They could not be assisted in any way, nor would they be permitted ever to sleep or eat indoors. Read that last sentence again and imagine what those boys were facing in the summer of 1911.

Entering Wyoming they were two days ahead of schedule. But Louis' horse died, the replacement wasn't a good traveler, and they hit the Pacific two days late. They'd averaged nearly 50 miles a day on horseback — a cross-country record that has never been equaled — and they won nothing. A few months later Indian gave the brothers a tandem motorcycle if they would repeat their ride from Oklahoma to New York City. They did, and then retired. Temple was seven.

Surely these boys are our spiritual ancestors, are they not? They weren't any more like the children of their era than we are like the motorcyclists of ours. But in the main they weren't doing long-distance rides in the sense we commonly use the phrase — SaddleSores, Bun Burners, and the like — although no one would question their unimaginable stamina.

So I return to the question: Having considered the exploits of two of the most remarkable riders who ever lived, how do we, their lineal descendants, define this thing that we do? Whatever that definition might be, it would almost certainly encompass this idea: At some point, you reach the last mile marker, the ride ends, and you can stop.

For one mythic traveler, however, that never happens. It is the *Flying Dutchman*, a ship condemned because of its captain's sacrilege forever to sail the seas, never to enter any harbor or refuge. I have recently met motorcycling's equivalent to this accursed ship, but before I introduce you to him, permit me to backtrack a moment.

Twenty years ago Merle Jacobsen wrote a weekly motor-cycle column for the *Washington Times* newspaper. During a casual conversation once, he mentioned that he was closing in on a perfect month. *A perfect* what? I asked. He explained that to him a perfect month was one in which he had ridden his bike at least one mile every single day.

I'd never thought of such a concept. But I'd been keeping track of every mile I'd ridden since 1990, so I checked if I'd ever had a perfect month. I did have, a few here and there, usually one a year. But in recent years I've been more focused. In 2004 I had five perfect months, seven each in 2005 and 2006, eight in 2007, and 10 in 2008. In 2009 I rode every day of the year through December 26. A perfect year was in reach. On December 27 I forgot to ride. I simply forgot.

When I realized what I'd done — or *not* done, in this case — on awakening on the morning of December 28, my first thought was to throw up. Then I laughed. Nothing I had achieved with my string of perfect months and almost perfect year could possibly compete with Blaine Paulus. I will tell you what he does, this Flying Dutchman of motorcycling; you tell me if this is endurance.

In the mid-1990s Paulus owned a small Moto Guzzi dealership in central Pennsylvania. An informal competition developed between him and some of the other dealers in the area to determine who could ride the most number of days in a year. In the winters north of Harrisburg it's often tough to wring out a perfect month. Paulus could win the annual challenge sometimes by riding just every other day. On February 20, 2000, he didn't ride at all. That was the last day of his life he wasn't on a bike for at least 10 miles.

That's a minimum of 10 miles, every day, every year. Snow, sleet, hail, driving rain, black ice. It doesn't matter. At least 10 more miles. He thought he might stop after 1,000 consecutive days. He rode 10 miles the next. Maybe 2,500 or 3,000 days in a row would be enough? Ten miles.

In the aftermath of one monster snowstorm, his wife looked out at a frozen tundra under two feet of snow as far as her eye could see. "I guess this is it," she said, shaking her head wistfully. It took him the better part of a day to plow a slippery path out to the highway. Access to the garage was impossible, but he had a small dirt bike in the basement. He and his son carried it upstairs, through the kitchen and living room, and out onto the porch. Ten more miles.

At some unknown point virtually everything in Blaine's life became condensed into getting those miles put away each day. He cannot crash out so badly he'll be hospitalized for an entire day; he cannot become so ill he's unable to ride 10 miles. No weather, flood, or atomic attack can be allowed to stop him. He's wary of traveling to Europe because the bike he might rent could break or be seized or rented to someone else. Until this endless string runs out, he'll never see Australia, New Zealand, or even Tahiti. The flight loses an entire day in the air westbound because of the international date line.

By the time you read this he'll have been on his bike every day for more than 4,500 straight days. He's ground out more than a million miles so far, many big days, many not. It was a milestone for him, that millionth one. But tonight he's just looking forward to the first 10 tomorrow. Nothing else counts. His ride has no end in sight.

Most of us who are in this loosely-knit club have a certificate or two on our wall or desk. There are no IBA awards for what the Abernathy boys and Blaine Paulus have managed to do, but they may be showing us by example what we otherwise have trouble analyzing and explaining. We're living in a big house, that's clear. It has a lot of dark, strange rooms.

I have to consider this problem further. Maybe I'll take the bike out. Ten miles sounds about right. Or I might learn to ride a horse.

[Postscript: As this book goes to press Blaine has completed his 19th consecutive perfect year. And so he sails on.]

Printed in Great Britain
by Amazon

82952402R00142